Welcome to the Jungle

A Frantic Journey Through
Motherhood and Self-Discovery

Anneliese Lawton

ISBN: 978-1-989506-57-8

Published in Canada by Pandamonium Publishing House™.
www.pandamoniumpublishing.com

Cover Design: Mary Pan and Alex Goubar

For my family: Mom, Dad, and Ricky.

Dave, Jack, Maxwell, and Abigail.

Thank you for gifting me with this beautiful life.

CONTENTS

FOREWORD

There's a desperate loneliness in early motherhood that no one tells you about. It's the loneliness of cradling a newborn while you're both still in diapers on a couch sagging with the weight of your constantly attached forms. It's the loneliness of looking around in bleary-eyed exhaustion with an aching neck and leaking boobs on the first day it's just the two of you and wondering, "What the hell happened to *my life*?"

It's the loneliness of snapping at your spouse in irrational, uncontrolled anger after he doesn't swaddle the baby to the standards your postpartum hormones demand. It's the loneliness of swiping away tears with the back of your hand as he storms out of the room and you hastily redo it yourself while thinking, "What the hell happened to *us*?"

It's the loneliness of depression, the isolation of anxiety, the shame and stigma of struggling just to get through each day when it looks so easy for everyone else. It's that small voice from deep within you that whispers, "What the hell happened to *me*?"

It's the loneliness of embarking on a journey that is completely universal yet somehow entirely, intimately, and uniquely *yours*—a journey that others can never fully comprehend because they are not you, and they are not mothering your child.

It's the loneliness of longing. Longing to be acknowledged, longing to be seen, longing to be held and reassured, but also longing to have some flippin' space from people needing you every moment of every hour of every day, thank you very much.

Welcome to the Jungle meets mothers in that loneliness. In that raw,vulnerable, hard, messy place, Anneliese Lawton takes off the filter and tears down the pretty window boxes to welcome you directly inside her *real*. Her *real* life. Her *real* motherhood. Her *real* marriage.Her *real* mental health. The real we all want to see, the real we all *need* to see, because it is a direct reflection of our own.

Anneliese is a kindred spirit—a fellow mom of two-under-two to whom I gravitated immediately because of her ability to "go there." She was writing down and sharing with the world all the gritty parts of motherhood that secretly brought me shame and guilt and despair in my own. But through her bravery and vulnerability, we unearthed an unbreakable bond founded on humor, self-acceptance, and genuine support.

With her stunningly heartfelt and honest storytelling, Anneliese shows us that it is only through our willingness to bare our souls and tell our authentic truths that we can truly find the connection that we crave as mothers. This is a book that every mother needs to read, a book that will have her nodding along, *Me, too*, a book that will feel like a beacon of light in some of the hardest and darkest places of her motherhood journey.

In *Welcome to the Jungle*, Anneliese will be there every step of the way, holding your hand and leading you out of the loneliness.

-Emily Solberg
(Her View from Home and Shower Thoughts with Emily Solberg)

INTRODUCTION

Parenting isn't for the faint of heart. It's also not for anyone who gets queasy at the sight of the three B's, blood, boogers, and barf. Since having three kids in just under four years, I've become well acquainted with the gross things that come out of other people's bodies. Including my own. Why didn't anyone warn me about lochia? When it comes to my kids, there's been split lips, stomach flus, and a little something my three-year-old likes to call "fart mess." If you know, you know. Parenthood, friends. It's a jungle. A fart-mess-covered jungle.

Mention the realities of parenthood out loud, and there's always a non-parent standing by with the "You signed up for this" spiel. They're not entirely wrong, I chose to have kids. Indeed, I did sign up for "this" in some way. You could even say I knew what I was getting into – but that would be a lie. I didn't know what I was getting into. Not all of it, anyway. Birth trauma and postpartum depression aren't exactly topics that come up in casual conversation. Unless you're like me – the queen of verbal diarrhea. No one *really* talks about the cold hard truth of parenting (and adulting and womanhood). Instead, we're expected to pull ourselves up by our bootstraps, quietly clean up the fart mess behind closed doors, and be dubbed the generation that's too weak if we show any emotion. What a way to form genuine, meaningful connections with other human beings.

Would it have changed anything if I knew about the realities of motherhood? Heck no. My kids – whose behaviours are questionable as fuck – are my everything. Their quirks, cute smiles, and sharp little puppy teeth are my pride and joy. I would give my life for them. But honesty has its place in parenting, and here's what I think it would have done for me…

If there was more honesty around the highs *and* lows of parenting, it would have told me that you're never truly ready to be a parent. There's never a perfect time. While you may think a stable career, loving relationship, and network of support are enough – parenting comes with a certain lack of control. Expect the unexpected. Anything can happen.

Honesty would have told me you never know who you'll get on the other end of that umbilical cord or what it will take to get a baby in your arms. Conceiving isn't always easy, pregnancy isn't always sunshine and rainbows, and sometimes…things go wrong. While you will love your child fiercely – no matter what – you may not have expected to be a statistic. Motherhood comes with grief and guilt, and a plethora of coping mechanisms that aren't always Dr. Phil-approved. You do what you can to survive.

Honesty would have also told me what kids do to a marriage – and that sometimes you'll seriously consider divorce. Some couples will actually get divorced. Sometimes a marriage can't be salvaged, despite one or both people in the relationship trying hard as fuck to save it. Illness, trauma, loss…career stress, financial woes… (and, thanks to our generational luck, a pandemic) can happen in a marriage. Throw in kids? Sheesh. Working to create a happy, loving, peaceful relationship is hard freaking work. Unbearable at times. Some relationships will see rock bottom. Some relationships will end up on the rocks because of sleep deprivation and the obnoxious way your partner chews. Pick your battles. And when you're running on two hours of sleep, expect those battles to become wars.

Another thing honesty would have told me is that my body would change. Not just because I gave birth but because my metabolism was going to come to a complete stop when I turned thirty. So, I'd have stretch marks, scars, and loose skin because I had a baby, but I would also start to worry about bone loss and collagen because I'm inching towards a free bus pass.

Honesty would have told me that my career would take on a life of its own because my priorities would change. I would contemplate the purpose of my work and how it compared to the privilege of raising my babies. While financial security would be important to me, I would desperately search for something more fulfilling than making money. A passion within me would ignite, pushing me to explore my individuality and granting me permission to chase my dreams. I would frantically pursue freedom and flexibility in my work to create some sort of "balance" with my family. Honestly would have told me that, eventually, I would find a career that made me feel accepted. Eventually, it would all work out – once I crawled out from under the piles and piles of diapers. I would come back from that career low, and I'd be better for it. Not because I would create the balance I desperately

3

sought, because balance is bullshit. But because I would find my passions and I would make something magical out of them. And while there would never be a balance between work and family, I would find solace in where I spent my time.

The most important thing honesty would have told me is that kids aren't the hard part of this entire scenario. Okay, that's a lie. There are moments my kids make me want to pull my hair out. Kids are hard. But another perspective is that they make life – which already comes with its own set of challenges – just a wee bit harder. Kids don't always give you the space to breathe, cope, or process adult things.

It's like that time my dog passed away. The puppy I snuck into the house when I was just eighteen. He was the puppy that tore up gardens and ate shoes. He barked each and every time the doorbell rang or when a bird flew past the window. He was the puppy my dad told me to "get rid of," and then fell hopelessly in love with him only weeks later. This puppy weaved his way into our little family unit and left footprints on our hearts. When we had to say goodbye, it was just my mom, dad, brother, and me. My original family unit. And then, after our goodbyes and tears and sharing memories that brought laughter, I returned home to my babies – where I went back on mom duty.

I grieved at home with my children while changing diapers, cooking dinners, and holding my babies through their tantrums. All while fighting back the tears. Being a mom doesn't always give you a break when things and life get hard. Often, you have to keep it all together to save face for your kids. Sometimes you need a moment inside a pantry to suck back a Snickers and cry into your sleeve. Sometimes you need a peaceful moment in the backyard broken up by your kids playing in the grass. And sometimes you need a hug from your husband when he walks in the door from work.

There are things that we expect to happen in life. But the way we've coped as a non-parent doesn't always work when you have a little one or two (or three) running around. For example, when you get the stomach flu. As much as some Gravol and a day in bed would do you some good, it's not going to happen. Instead, your toddler will treat you as a mechanical bull and "yeehaw" while sitting on your back while you puke your brains out. Or the devastating moment you lose your own parent. You'll get to a place where you think you have your grief under control. And then one Sunday while collecting rocks, your four-year-old will ask you where grandpa went, and you'll be thrown right back into it. Maybe you'll wake up on the wrong side of the bed one morning because stress from work kept you up all night. Being a parent means you can't crawl back under those soft sheets. Your kid wants pancakes shaped like a bunny for breakfast.

You love your kids. You want their childhood to be perfect. So, you barf with them on your back, talk about grandpa in heaven and make dinosaur-shaped pancakes because they hated the bunny ones you made first. And at the end of a long day, you crawl into bed and collapse because you're exhausted from navigating parenthood, adulthood, and humanhood all in one. So yes, kids are hard – but parents are human, and navigating human things that are a part of everyday life, is hard, too.

I decided to have kids. I expected it would come with ups and downs. I just didn't expect everyone to be so hush, hush about the less-than-picture-perfect moments that come along with parenting, specifically being a mother. And when it comes to raising children, I think that's one of the most challenging parts of the whole darn thing. That there's this shame around not loving every moment. But we can love our children and still find that we need time away from them every now and then. We can love being a mother and still find moments where our children test our patience. We can share candidly about depression and disappointments without being shamed for feeling anything but pure joy. But sometimes, it's hard for society to see mothers as more than just mothers. There's this expectation that we wear our motherhood as a badge of honour without acknowledging the reality that women are raising children in a society that celebrates work over rest, productivity over peace, and output over joy. Mothers are burning out. And I'm tired of raising babies in a society that expects women to be everything for everyone. It's not just women who would benefit from feeling supported in motherhood; children will benefit, too.

As I've lived and bred children in the deepest parts of the jungle, I've grown an animalistic instinct to protect my babies – an animalistic instinct to protect the sacredness of the life my husband and I have created. I've grown into an untamed mama bear who loudly advocates for my children and, more recently, myself. It's foreign to me. I've never lived so loudly in my life. I used to be shy and timid. I hardly spoke to my own friends, let alone share my deepest feelings with strangers. But the person I am today prefers to be vulnerable. I think becoming more resilient and fostering better connections with others is needed. When we feel connected to other people and have positive relationships in our life, it boosts our self-esteem and helps make space for more self-love.

Imagine it. A life where it's acceptable to wear your heart on your sleeve. A life where you don't have to hide your struggles – a life where talking about them actually connects you with people who can understand and support you. It's the only life that works for me. And yet, some people still can't wrap their heads around it.

I used to think playing it close to your chest was a generational thing – but even within my own generation, it's pretty taboo. "Annie said WHAT on social media?" "That girl really needs to keep her private life private." "Is she trying to be the next Meghan Markle or something?" A family member said that. She told my husband that my parenting blog was my attempt at becoming the next Meghan Markle. If the tone isn't clear – they implied it as a bad thing. Yes, this family member believed that I, Anneliese Lawton of Ontario, Canada, was blogging in an attempt to become Meghan Markle, the Duchess of freaking Sussex. A woman with notable charitable work and patronages under her belt. If my mental health musings on a little Facebook blog have earned me a comparison to the global ambassador for World Vision Canada, then I'll wear that badge proudly…along with the Meghan Markle t-shirt I bought to wear to our next family gathering. I'm shallow like that.

The older generation, and even some of my own, simply don't get the open and honest thing. And that's okay – because I believe vulnerability is the driving force of connection and the key to close relationships. I want that in my life and for my children – close relationships with a foundation built on trust and understanding. I want others to feel brave to do the same, only if they feel called. I'm not asking you to bare the deepest parts of your soul. But I would like to create an awareness that everyone is carrying some baggage or trauma with them. We have no idea what's going on behind closed doors. Sometimes we see that baggage or trauma come to life in a triggered moment. A friend could be short or impatient. A stranger could appear grumpy and withdrawn. As a general rule, we should always be kind to one another because you never know when you're catching someone on an off day.

I write about things most people would never dare to discuss so candidly, specifically mental health. And when I hit publish on my first blog, a family member told me to shut my mouth. Seriously. She's from an older generation and not exactly in touch with her feelings (she's also the person who called me Meghan Markle). She told me she couldn't support me in airing my dirty laundry. Emotions are meant to be kept private. Putting everything on display for the world to see is embarrassing. I should keep my feelings where they belong – at home – and cry on the shoulder of someone in my immediate circle. Only if I needed it…which I shouldn't…because women should deal with this type of stuff alone.

Whew. That was a tough pill to swallow. I nearly walked away from writing about my life with depression and motherhood altogether. This woman wasn't being asked to share her story. Instead, she was trying to keep me from telling mine. As I blossomed into who I truly wanted to be, she continued to meet me with resistance at every turn.

Full disclosure: I spew my private life left, right, and center. Or, I guess, what you would modernly call: Facebook, Instagram, and TikTok. I'm pretty transparent about divulging the good, the bad, and the hilarious regarding parenting and mental health. I feel like it's my civic duty to remain truthful about, well, the doodie. Though, for a long while, I only put the keyboard to the screen for me. My Facebook blog – *Grown Up Glamour by Anneliese Lawton* – was a place for me to reflect on pregnancy, babyhood, and toddler years. A digital journal. In that space, I shared with my heart on my sleeve, as raw and authentically as if you were living the tale alongside me in my living room. Which I can now say I've welcomed tens of thousands of other parents into.

There was one post that was the inspiration behind this book. In less than five minutes I threw together three hundred words about my experience with my maternal health and my belief that mothers fall through the cracks of our healthcare system without adequate mental health support after the birth of their child. In less than 24 hours, the post went viral. Within a week, it was translated into seven different languages reaching over six million people. Six million mothers nodded in unison and solidarity. But what if I kept my mouth shut like that family member told me I should? Would those women have ever felt validated? Where would I be today if I hadn't told my story? Or shared the truth of my experience? If I had kept my mouth shut. The truth is – I would never have healed. I still would have been fighting my depression. I wouldn't be living life as my authentic self. I would've made the same mistake time and again throughout my life. If I had listened to the critics in my life, I can tell you that you wouldn't be holding my book in your hands today.

Putting yourself out there the way I do, results in lots of negative feedback. Of course, sharing the most vulnerable pieces of yourself brings out the trolliest of trolls. The good far outweighs the bad. Even if my words touch one person while ten others find a reason to criticize me, there's one more person in this world who has felt heard and validated. And that goes for you too. Whatever you're being called to, it's because it's bigger than you. Once you start acting on your deepest desires, validation will come. Sure, there may be trolls, but there's something about feeling validated that ignites a fire in you to keep carrying on.

You don't have to listen to the advice or guidance of anyone but yourself. Your inner voice is the only one that matters. And I'm talking about that authentic inner voice – not the yappy negative one that sounds like your worst critic. Your inner voice is that nudge pushing you toward what feels right (even if it feels scary).

Motherhood stripped me naked and forced me to figure out who I am. And while I've had imposter syndrome and insecurities, and while I've quit blogging about motherhood a time or seven, I finally found my place in this big ole world. And it's all because of them, my babies.

1

WHEN WHITE PANTS WERE COOL

Short, awkward – a little bit smelly – and thirteen. It's the age I got my first training bra, the age I had my first kiss, and the age I realized I wasn't "enough." Celebrities with perfectly curved bodies were enough. Britney Spears and Christina Aguilera were desirable in every way. Something about them distorted my thoughts and triggered a deeper fear of unacceptance. Then, there were three Laurens. The dynamic trio of St. Paul's Catholic Elementary. They were enough. Popular, blonde, and desirable. Not me; I wasn't cool, pretty, or smart. My hair was untamed, my legs were hairy, and my teeth had railroad tracks plastered to them. I was rejected and unwanted. Facing a harrowing struggle – a quest – to figure out what others had that I didn't. I knew it came down to looks. I didn't have them. I wasn't enough, and enough is all I ever wanted to be.

My frantic journey toward becoming enough started within the white cinderblock walls of my eighth-grade math class. Mr. Celine was scratching word problems onto the chalkboard. Wretched word problems. I could never wrap my head around them. The combination of numbers and letters disoriented my thinking. As I copied the day's assignment with my fuzzy pink pencil, a note casually floated between my peers. Hand-to-hand. Each time Mr. Celine turned to face the board, the note would exchange. Passing between the Laurens and the Zacks, it slowly made its way to my desk. I had never received a note in class before. I wasn't one of those girls. I didn't have many friends, wasn't in with the 'cool' crowd, and was far too awkward to have any sort of secret admirer. The note travelled closer.

As it landed in my corner of the room, I could see my name doodled on the top in red ink. I peeked at my best friend, the only person it could come from. The only person who ever really spoke to me. Well, that's not totally true. Other kids in my class talked to me. They would say things like, "Hey! Hairy Gorilla! Lift your shirt." Or, "Ew! Why do you smell like vinegar?" That one is on my mom. (As an adult, I've learned vinegar is her secret sauce to a squeaky-clean load of laundry.) I wouldn't say the kids in my class didn't like me. They never took the time to get to know me. And how can you dislike someone if you've never even attempted to speak to them? Instead, I was a glaring target. Teased and tormented for my unique approach to fashion and old-school family values. Like on Pizza Day when the popular boy spat on my lunch. He also wrote, "Annie is a dirtbag," on his pencil case and passed it around for the whole class to see. Just like the note. I was chased home, laughed at, and put in awkward situations that were meant to make me stand out.

With eagerness and anticipation, I peeled back the edges of the note, finding the same red pen scribbled under the flaps.

It read:

"Um, I just think you should know a lot of people don't

like you." The writing was my best friend's, and she had a heart beside the period. Because it's hard to blame the messenger when they add a heart, right?

I could feel the skin on my greasy, pubescent face turn red as I sank into my chair. My breathing grew heavy, and my mind panicked. Everyone was looking at me; I could feel it. Despite the silence in the room, I could hear familiar laughter echoing off the white brick walls. I slouched in my chair and lowered my head, trying to disappear into a room full of equally awkward students. I refused to look up and give them what they wanted - my vulnerability. My heart raced faster as I desperately searched for an escape. Raising my hand, I excused myself to the bathroom to seek refuge in the stall. It was safe there, among the toilets and the paper towels. It was a safe space to cry. Hiding anonymously behind the speckled pink door where no one could see my weakness.

As a thirteen-year-old girl, nothing was more important to me than having friends and fitting in, especially since I had just moved to a new neighbourhood and started a new school. At that impressionable age, acceptance defined my self-worth – and without acceptance, I had no reason to value myself.

Before thirteen, the 'in crowd' was never a place I felt excluded from as it was never a place I yearned to be. I made friends easily before my parents picked up and moved across town, placing me at a new, more affluent school with new peers to fit in with. It wasn't really a place I belonged. Most parents of my peers were white collar and worked corporate jobs. My parents scrimped and saved every penny they made on a single blue-collar income. While some kids were dropped off at school in an Audi or even a newer Toyota, our family drove a ten-year-old Ford

Aerostar. I stood out in the crowd before I even made my way through the school doors.

Now that I was thirteen and at a new school, things felt different. The girls were mature; they had boyfriends, and they wore bras and thongs. They were nothing like the girls from my old school who had been by my side since the age of four. My old friends were the type of girls who made me feel safe, and they were the type of girls who would never send me a note telling me I was unlikeable.

Around the time I received the note, my best friend had started kissing boys and finding her way in with the popular crowd. At that age, kissing boys was risqué; it grabbed attention…it made you cool.

Kissing boys was something very foreign to me. I was still coming to terms with the fact that Santa didn't exist. A gut-wrenching revelation. Something I'm still not sure I'm ready to accept to this day. I was also raised in a somewhat reserved household. My mother is Italian and Roman Catholic, so you can imagine the Catholic guilt and fear of God that influenced my actions anytime a boy walked in my direction. I usually ran the other way.

I was an easy target for this new crowd of confident teen girls and boys. The new girl, who still played with dolls, rode her bike and wore high-rise underwear that covered her ass cheeks.

However, my best friend was determined to turn this around for me – the whole nobody liking me thing – all for my benefit, of course. She took me under her wing and promised to show me the ropes. First, I had to change my clothes and hair; more than anything, I had to ditch my innocence, including my belief in Santa Claus.

But I knew I could only make these changes with help from the bank of mom and dad... I mean, at thirteen, they still bought my underwear. I didn't care if I had to seek spiritual support from the Father, the Son, and the Holy Spirit; I was determined to get them on board with my dream to acquire a new and improved look.

The next time my mom and I went to the mall, I veered from the pre-teen stores. They were too young and immature; they wouldn't have what I was trying to find. I was becoming a woman. I was going to kiss boys. I couldn't wear shirts with puppies anymore; I needed something cool – something sexy. I didn't want to stand out; in fact, I tried to blend in with every single girl in my class. Tank tops, tight jeans, Phat Farm shoes – that's what I needed.

As I shuffled through the racks, I pulled out tops that would expose my belly and jeans that would sit just below my hips. The early 2000s low-rise hip-huggers. Britney Spears *rocked* them.

I brought at least a dozen items into the changing room that day. Everything from low-rise blue jeans to ruffle crop tops and even a pair of platform shoes. After all, this was the Spice Girl's decade, and I was about to spice up my life.

I distinctly remember falling in love with a pair of tight white paints with the word "Angel" written on the bum. They were *everything*. And, of course, paired perfectly with a black crop top with "Virgo" bedazzled across the chest. If it's not completely obvious, your girl's zodiac sign is Virgo (the symbol for a Virgo is 'Virgin', which is also incredibly fitting). I completed the ensemble with a pair of platform shoes and clip-in crimped hair. I was a vision – sure to be the envy of the schoolyard.

I can still see my mom's face when I came out of that changing room. I think she placed a collect call to Jesus. My mom does not hide her feelings very well – she thinks she does – but she doesn't. I could see it written all over her face. This outfit was going to be an *oh hell no*. But I had to convince her I wasn't her little girl anymore – I was a teenager. And I was sexy. The girls at school were going to love this. Not to mention the boys.

My mom swiped her credit card with hesitation and prayer on her Rosary. She bought me the clothes, and I think it's because a part of her could understand. My mom started school at the age of five as an immigrant. Not only did she hardly speak English, but she also wore clothes handmade by my Nonna. Something to be cherished, yes. But something to fit in with kids at school? Hard no. She understood what it was like to be singled out, and she did her best to help me through this critical period in my development while encouraging me to be true to myself. A concept that's really hard to grasp when all you want to do is be someone else to fit in.

Remaining true to myself. It's a concept my mom has shoved down my throat each day of my life. And only now, as I try to find my way back to that person, can I understand why.

I never took my mom's advice not to change myself for others. And despite my best efforts to change my clothes, hair, and personality, I was never accepted into the 'it crowd'…and I lost my identity trying.

That note – about being unlikeable – was a cruel

awakening to the life I had to navigate as a woman. A life where I would have to be someone I'm not in order to play nice and meet the expectations set by others. A life where I would veer so far from my identity trying to fit a mold that I would lose who I was in the process. "A lot of people don't like you."

Those words changed the course of my life. This statement became my mantra. For me, the note was more than just social acceptance. It was the pivotal moment when I decided that everything I knew myself to be wasn't good enough.

That day in eighth-grade math was the first day I surrendered a piece of myself to make room for a piece of someone else. It was also the first time I experienced what I would learn to be an anxiety attack. Anxiety would eventually become my security blanket. I would use it as a way to excuse myself from reaching for people, places, and things that truly set my soul on fire. I grew so afraid of rejection that I wouldn't even try.

From that day in eighth-grade math to motherhood, I lost significant pieces of my identity. I lost friendships, my dreams and aspirations, and the truest and most beautiful version of myself. I became a piece of Swiss cheese over the course of my life, riddled with holes. The only way I was able to find my way back was by hitting rock bottom. A long and drawn-out fifteen-year journey of giving in to peer pressure, making poor decisions, and ignoring the little whispers from inside. Today, I know those years were all a part of the plan. The hurt and the anguish were all part of my bigger picture. For me, that could only come to fruition when I found myself lost in the only role I believed would complete me – motherhood. It was only in this role that I would find my way back to myself.

2

HYPER-FIXATING FIXES THINGS…RIGHT?

I don't know if it was just me, but I used to think any boy who looked in my direction was "The One." There was Brett in kindergarten, Simon in grade six, and my boyfriend at seventeen. Their potential was confirmed with a game of MASH and a cootie catcher. We were going to have six kids, drive a rocket ship, and live in a church. The science behind it was solid.

"The One" didn't come into my life until my early twenties – and on paper, the outcome is a cookie-cutter family: three kids, an SUV, and a house in suburbia. Maybe one day we'll ride on our very own rocket – but for now, a mode of transportation with ample trunk space is critical. Truly, my life is everything I ever dreamed of. But there was a placeholder boyfriend there for a while who also happened to be my first experience with love.

I was seventeen when love walked into my life for the first time. And it came in the form of a nineteen-year-old hockey player with tight abs and a Honda Civic. You could hear his car coming from a mile away. It was the traditional mating call of teenage boys in the early 2000s. And panties dropped. If I only knew that one day, my heart would stop for a 30-year-old man wearing spiderman underwear on his head while fighting spaghetti monsters on a Saturday morning. Man, things change. But then, there was nothing more appealing to a seventeen-year-old girl than a boyfriend who could buy his own beer and had his own set of obnoxious wheels. It reeked of freedom and Axe body spray. I was hooked.

While I was with this young man – all my insecurities seemed to disappear. He wasn't from my high school and didn't know my history – and therefore, I believe he saw me for who I was, cute, quirky, and shy. Because he was older, he made me feel "taken care of." It was the perfect storm. I quickly saw the benefits of dating someone a few years ahead in the game. Someone more world-wise. High school was coming to a close, and I was about to enter that world. He would take my hand and lead me there with a protective cloak and a road map.

Falling in love at seventeen was like biting into a good piece of chocolate cake. It was sweet, fluffy, and just a bit dense—just two foolish teens spending the summer together and having fun. But when school started in the fall, we didn't part ways like we had planned. Instead, the intoxicating combination of his attention and potential was like the first dose of an addiction. And while I knew it might not be my life's best or deepest love, I kept returning for more.

In my pursuit of higher education (and a taste of freedom), I applied to a handful of universities between two to five hours away from home—the one I chose was one right in the middle. The campus sat along a beautiful winding river with forests on either side of the grounds. The school was small and cozy –most importantly, it was a three-hour drive from home. Far enough so I'd have to live on campus but close enough to bring my laundry home on weekends when I ran out of clean underwear.

As I packed up the contents of my pretty pink bedroom and devoured every last piece of my mama's homemade pasta, the realities of my decision began to weigh. The chapter of my childhood was closing. For the first time, I wouldn't wake up to the sound of my mom scrambling eggs the floor below. I wouldn't share a couch with my dad on Saturdays for Hockey Night in Canada. I wouldn't have my brother to save my butt after drunken teenage escapades. This was it. I was leaving my childhood home and joining the big 'ole world. My life was about to begin.

I would also be leaving another piece of me behind. The boy I had grown to love over those summer months—a boy who would be returning to his school on the other side of Lake Ontario. So, in a last-ditch effort to seal the deal, I erased any evidence of childhood altogether and said goodbye with the most important piece of me.

My virginity wasn't just important to me – my virginity *was* me. In high school, I had grown a reputation for being the girl who wouldn't give it up. My virginity was something sacred and I wanted to keep it until I got married – or at least until I knew I was with "The One."

Society teaches girls that their virginity is precious and incredibly valuable to have. We're damaged if we lose it the wrong way or at the wrong time. If we have sex for any other reason than loving our partner, we're sluts. Young girls are taught that sex shouldn't be a casual or speedy affair. We're taught sex is for someone you love and want to spend the rest of your life with. And having lost my virginity under that pretense, I've come to believe that messaging isn't anything but dangerous.

My deep desire to remain abstinent was primarily influenced by Catholic guilt and my exposure to the teachings in the Bible. Subconsciously, I think my insecurities played a role in my decision-making too. Despite my cute personality, tiny waist, and unassuming beauty, I was wildly insecure. After being teased and tormented in my preteens, I never really outgrew the idea that my body was ugly and nobody wanted to be my friend. I think I knew that when I gave up my virginity, I'd be giving up the only piece of myself that I had control over. The Catholic church made me feel it was the only thing about myself that mattered. Somehow, I knew that if I handed it over to someone else, I'd never be able to walk away from the relationship. I knew that even if the relationship was the worst thing for me, I would do whatever I could to make it work because it was what the Catholic church expected of me. It's what I came to expect of me.

As a first-year student in a university town, Frosh week was an eye-opening experience. There was drinking, sex, and fake I.Ds. Among a million other things, I'd never seen before. Back home, I'd heard rumors that people could funnel a twenty-sixer of vodka, but now I had seen it with my own eyes. It was an out-of-body experience. Everyone walked around campus with Mike's Hard Lemonade and Brava beer, playing flip-cup and rolling joints. There were friends to be made, boys to be loved, and textbooks of information to be absorbed. But with my boyfriend and my virginity four hours away – I couldn't commit to the life I had chosen before I fell in love.

With my focus on only one thing – him – I let the potential of what could have been completely slip away –

and eventually, I dropped out of my first year of university, changed my major, applied to another university, and chased my boyfriend across the pond. We spent the next three years bringing out the worst in each other.

Then after four years of dating, arguing, threatening to leave, getting back together again, planning our life, and infidelity accusations – we broke up two weeks after university ended. That formative chapter where you're supposed to find your lifelong friends, set yourself up for success in your career, and really come into your own passed me by. And I didn't have anything but a broken heart to show for it.

That breakup was one of the first times I hyper-fixated to cope. The man I ended up marrying has come to know this hyper-fixation well. It's a thing I do when I've completely lost control over my surroundings. I find it empowering, though it's usually counterproductive. My husband hates when I hyper-fixate – because my hyper-fixations mean his to-do list gets longer. When I was on my first mat leave and felt trapped within the four walls of my home, I hyper-fixated on painting—and moving furniture. Which resulted in my husband painting the remaining walls and putting furniture back in its place. When we got pregnant with our second son only eight months after having our first, I hyper-fixated on moving. My husband did odd jobs around the house to make me stay. When I spontaneously quit my job one sunny Tuesday, I hyper-fixated on starting my own business. My husband pulled up his bootstraps and supported his mentally unstable wife in every way. I hyper-fixate. It's my thing. It's the reason behind my incredible work ethic and success, but it's also one of my most negative traits. This hyper-fixation creates a painful loop in my mind where I berate myself with the idea that what I'm doing, what I have, and who I am is not enough.

The only way for me to be enough is to overachieve, over-accomplish, and overcome the challenges in my life at an unrealistic pace.

With my first love behind me and regrets weighing on me heavily, I tried to become the best damn version of myself. All to make my first love eat his dust and regret his decision to leave me behind. I wanted to be the one that got away. He was the boyfriend I lost my virginity to. He was the boyfriend I sacrificed my education for. He was the boyfriend I chased. That core group of friends you make in college and university? I didn't even attempt to make them – because all I needed was him. So, when my world came crashing down after he walked out, I was utterly alone.

It was only when I found myself alone that it hit me – you will not find happiness by chasing someone else's. For nearly a decade, I had changed myself for others and followed the status quo. And after all that, I was still alone.

In a desperate attempt to put the pieces of myself back together, I hyper-fixated on the things that could push me forward. I channeled every ounce of my energy into volunteering, networking, hanging out with my old hometown friends, and being unapologetically me. I was going to become the type of woman every man would desire.

Then without warning, my world came crashing down with an unforeseen diagnosis and halted my plans for the future. A new type of hyper-fixation was about to begin.

At twenty-one, just as my boyfriend walked out of my life, polycystic ovarian syndrome (PCOS) walked in. A devastating disorder with the power to take away my fertility. And just like that, the future I dreamed of was gone.

As I picked up the pieces of my broken heart, I pivoted my fixation. Instead of being the best version of myself, I began to fixate on my future. I fixated on my fertility. I frantically tried to control an uncontrollable situation—no one my age was planning for children as strategically as I was. Every relationship was an opportunity to have the answer. Every potential suitor held the key. I had to find the person who would be entirely on board with the unknown. The only way I knew how to protect myself was to be transparent. Every date, every relationship – I laid it all on the table. I may not be able to have a baby.

A desperate desire to have a baby isn't exactly first-date talk. Especially at twenty-one-with people you've just met. But having a baby or not having a baby, consumed me. All I could think about was my future family and what PCOS would mean for my future husband. All the pressure to have a baby was on me. It is a woman's job to bear children (this is what I told myself). Would a man find me to be enough without my fertility and my virginity? There were only two outcomes here: my body would fail me, or it wouldn't fail me. Until I tried to make a baby, I wouldn't honestly know. So, I needed to find someone who was in it for me. Someone who found me to be enough. Then, together, we would try to do the baby thing.

3

FIRST COMES LOVE

I met my husband the old-fashioned way, in the parking lot of a local bar after too many beers. Not on Tinder, Match.com, or any of the other modern ways of dating – although sometimes we both feel we missed out on the thrill of finding each other by swiping right. He was handsome, I had liquid courage, and the rest was history. At least, that's how Dave tells it. My version is a little more *Cinderella* and a little less *Wedding Crashers*.

Dave and I both did our first love thing from the last year of high school until just after university graduation. Important and formative years. We missed out on the same experiences and held the same regrets. After years of lessons learned at the hands of the young and naive (and the formation of our frontal lobe), we managed to find our way to each other. Here's my favourite part of our story, we would only find one another because of first love. It had its place and purpose in our lives. I believe it always does. Young first love is a training ground for adult intimacy and a space to experience strong emotions. You learn about the importance of communication and patience. It doesn't go without saying, pieces of you usually get lost along the way. But if you can find the strength to move forward and grow and apply lessons learned in your future relationships, it's only a matter of time before magic is made. I'd find my magic in Dave – and in finding him, I'd learn a valuable lesson about timing…and, maybe, fate.

By logic, Dave and I should've met long before we actually had. We travelled in the same circle, went to the same weddings and parties, and even grew up in the same neighbourhood, just streets away from each other.

Fate was patiently waiting for the perfect time to bring us together. This is probably a good thing…because I believed in Santa Claus until I was thirteen…and Dave, well, he had a reputation for being a little bit of a bad boy. Had we met any sooner, we both would have run for the hills.

My twenty-second birthday was when the stars would align. I was sitting in a local bar with a group of my closest friends, chit-chatting over a gourmet meal of nachos and beer. My friends Ian and Katie blabbed on about some guy their friend had just broken up with. He had blonde hair and brown eyes. He was intellectual. Most importantly, he was kind. Ian and Katie promised – with crossed hearts – he had potential. I thought he sounded almost too good to be true. So, fate played its card and decided it was time. The two of us were far enough away from believing in Santa and causing small-scale havoc on the streets to finally meet. Dave lived a few cities away at the time, but as my friends and I left the bar, he walked in. Brown hair, brown eyes, just as handsome as I had pictured him. And my goodness, was he kind. The rest is history.

After that night, Dave and I were almost inseparable. Except for the two months early in our relationship when we broke up. Can you guess why? My frantic need for honesty. After about two weeks of dating and a few too many tallboys at a Blue Jays game, I told my new, agnostic boyfriend that, as a Catholic, I needed to get married in a church. There wasn't any way around it. The next day my new boyfriend told me it wasn't going to work. It wasn't me; it was him. He wasn't ready to get serious with someone so fast. I mean – wedding bells? I don't blame him.

While Dave ended our relationship, he didn't walk out of my life. We stayed friends, and we spoke every day. Within our friendship, I found comfort, and eventually, I told him about my PCOS. He had the wit to respond by telling me he didn't like his genes that much anyway. I was falling in love: hook, line, and sinker. And eventually, he felt the same about me. Four years later, Dave dropped to one knee and asked me to be his wife.

There are only a handful of days you remember like it was yesterday—the birth of your children, the death of a loved one, the night of your wedding. The night my husband proposed is one of them, too. There's something about a strong, confident man wobbling at the knees, sweating and vulnerable, that you simply can't forget.

It was a cold December night, and Dave made plans for us to travel into the city to the Toronto Christmas Market. Snow had freshly fallen, Christmas was weeks away, and the sky twinkled with lights. He grabbed my hands, and despite the cold, his palms were sweaty (knees weak, arms are heavy). Under a starlit city sky, he led me down a cobblestone path with the snow crunching beneath our feet. We walked past the vendor booths – the smell of cinnamon and hot apple cider in the air – towards a beautifully lit white spruce towering in the center of the Distillery District. Standing there in awe, taking in the sights, sounds, and smells, Dave tucked me between the tree branches, placing us out of the market chaos. It was there, between the soft needles and warm white lights, where he dropped to one knee and asked me to marry him. Knees in the snow, looking up at me with his big brown eyes; my forever after, asked me to be his wife. My heart filled with butterflies as I looked back down at this man, the man I would get to do life with. The man I would fight to have a family with. The man who found me to be enough.

I believed Dave and I would conquer anything life would throw our way – and that's because of him. He has a way of remaining calm, positive, and optimistic. Watching him stay composed while my mind spins in every direction about things that can go wrong is incredibly annoying. Hopefully, our kids' coping mechanisms will be somewhere in the middle between the two of us. With the perfect balance of worry and composure to navigate life easily while also being a realist. Dave is also the type of person whose sense of humor parallels Jerry Seinfeld. His humor is based on the commonplace aspects of everyday life. Life with him was destined and has proven to be endlessly funny and uplifting, even when shit hits the fan. Which has happened often in our life together.

Nine months after the perfect Christmas proposal, we said "I do" at our 1920's themed wedding. Our big, beautiful family surrounded us in a big, beautiful church. And yes, it rained.

4

SORRY FOLKS, MARRIAGE IS HARD

The first year of marriage isn't the hardest. And if
you think it is, you're probably still in your first year of
marriage. Sure, if you haven't lived together, there's the
combining of finances, working around two careers, shared
engagements, and feeling the reality of married life. Not
to mention the millennial starter pack, which includes a
rising cost of living, combined school debt, having enough
personal space – the toilet seat being up or down – there's a
lot to figure out.

Our friends and family thought Dave and I were fast-
tracking a divorce when we decided to try to have a baby
within our first year of marriage. Very non-millennial of us.
Our friends were still travelling the world, pursuing their
careers, and exploring an assortment of partners – the fun
stuff you do in your twenties. Many close to us believed
we were setting ourselves up for failure. I mean, we were
trading in travelling and parties for diapers. I can kind
of see their point. Your twenties are when you're fully
equipped to live your best life – you have a disposable
income, and free time, there's nothing really holding you
back. We chose to go in the other direction. We signed up

for the stressful as fuck starter pack.

Immediately after our honeymoon, Dave came with me to my doctor to figure out what it would take for me to get pregnant. Many couples who experience infertility or difficulty conceiving don't have a heads-up. In fact, many go through at least a year of trying before a doctor will even take their fertility seriously. A year filled with torture and loss and sex penciled into a calendar. Not many couples go into starting their family with what we knew – that it might not work. To try to ease some of the stress, we looked for answers. What would happen if we couldn't have a baby?

Dave and I sat in my doctor's office, hand-in-hand, with optimism and anxiety pulsing through our veins. I think I was more anxious than Dave. I know I was, always have been, and always will be. He's a go-with-the-flow kind of guy. He was okay with whatever would happen, from not having a baby to navigating fertility treatments to adoption. For me, a baby was everything. While I was open to adoption, something about creating little versions of my husband and me seemed romantic. Despite my husband being flexible with our outcome, I put pressure on myself to provide him with his genetic heir. I wanted to create something with him. And society made me feel like anything besides a genetic baby between us, meant that I would be failing my husband (and my own parents) in my womanly duties. Which certainly isn't the case. And while I didn't experience infertility, I imagine there have been other women who have also felt the same pressure in their journey. If having our own baby didn't work out, I was convinced I would die.

My doctor went over the stats of conceiving with PCOS. Infertility in women with PCOS varies, and while most women become pregnant, they often take longer to conceive and are more likely to need fertility treatments. Some things could increase our chances: exercise and healthy eating – everything I loathed. But, with a diagnosis already under wraps, we were one step ahead in the game. The best course of action was to try for six months. If it didn't work out, we'd move on to a fertility clinic.

I desperately wanted a family, whatever it would take. Dave was less frantic but promised to support me every step of the way. *What will be, will be.*

Like many couples, Dave and I have our fault lines, but through our love and vows, we were determined to overcome whatever landed in our path, even if it included infertility.

Since that first year of marriage, we've been through the fucking wringer. Being a little older and wiser now, we've learned that you can't predict what life will bring or how hard it will be. More importantly, you can't always predict how you'll respond to those challenging moments.

Thanks to first love (and another shout-out to that fully-formed frontal lobe), Dave and I entered our relationship with clear boundaries and expectations. Communication, understanding, and support were all essential qualities we valued and happened to find in one another. We could also shake each other out of any situation when things got hard. We were able to lean on each other in weak moments. But we hadn't even skimmed the surface of what was to come. With bits of me already broken when I entered our marriage, and with a big part of me still not knowing who I was, I'm confident in saying my mental health wasn't prepared for what our marriage would face.

Within the first year of our union, we learned that marriage doesn't always look pretty beyond the altar. By year three, it's a blessing that we didn't have a divorce lawyer on speed dial. However, the day we said, "I do," we couldn't imagine anything more than a few minor hiccups along our way to forever.

I remember our vows. We looked at each other with hope. We beamed at one another with love passionately pumping through our veins. With Dave's hands in mine and mine in his, we sealed our love with a promise and a kiss.

'I take thee, my love, to be my wedded husband or wife, to have and to hold from this day forward, for better, for worse, for richer, for poorer, in sickness and in health, to love and to cherish, till death do us part.'

On October 3, 2015, we recited our vows and meant them. But we wanted to get to the good stuff. To the party. To the wedding night. Standing hand-in-hand at the church, we didn't process how powerful our vows were and that our marriage would completely change when faced with sickness, health, better or worse. And sometimes, life as we knew it would never be the same.

Over the last seven years, I've learned that marriage is more than a white dress and a black tuxedo. It's more than promising to love your spouse through thick and thin. Marriage is beyond anything you imagined when you sealed your love with a kiss and a certificate.

Through the ups and downs of life, I've learned the difference between love and marriage. A marriage won't always be steady. Vows become actions (and sometimes inactions). A lifetime together comes with loss, illness, and hardships. In a marriage, you'll go weeks without sex or sleep, and somehow, some way, you have to find the patience to tolerate one another. It's literally sickness, health, and everything in between.

I've also learned about love. Love can get foggy when a marriage grows tired. It's what feels easy in those moments when a marriage is strong. Love as a feeling goes away when circumstances change. Love as a verb is an unconditional commitment. Love is changing your wife's postpartum pad as she aches over a toilet. Wiping your husband's tears as he mourns over the loss of his father. Love is much more than marriage. It's more than a day of celebration and a certificate binding your relationship under the law. Love is sharing all of life's experiences together, it's managing the unexpected, it's saying 'I do' every morning, every night, and sometimes every minute of the day. Marriage is legally binding. But love, my friends, love is a choice you make each and every day.

For Dave and me, the first year of marriage was hard. Not for the reasons one would think. Not because of bills, jobs, or any of the traditional first year of marriage woes. It was because getting pregnant turned out to be easier than we expected. We conceived during our second month of trying, which was our second month of marriage. We had a too-good-to-be-true experience. And then, at twelve weeks pregnant, our world fell apart, and we learned the responsibility we held as parents. Even then, our first year of marriage wasn't the hardest. It was our third. The third year of marriage was when our vows were truly put to the test.

It's impossible to predict what will happen in life. And when you're standing at that altar looking into the eyes of the person you want to spend life with, it's impossible to predict where your marriage will end up, despite your best intentions to keep it intact. There are so many outliers, and it's no question that relationships are complicated. And despite your common ground of creating and loving your children together, raising children within marriage is complicated. There will be times you and your partner align in movie-worthy happy-family moments, and there will be moments when you wonder what you ever saw in each other when you first fell in love all those years ago. You'll come head-to-head when you find yourselves on opposite ends of parenting strategies. And when intimacy becomes something scheduled into a calendar rather than a spontaneous moment of love. It's when your self-esteem chips away because of physical or emotional changes or when communication and patience grow tired. Your marriage gets complicated when the only way you can cope with the overstimulation in your life is by withdrawing from your partner. With children in the picture, it gets really hard to recognize the person you married, let alone yourself.

During our first years together, before becoming parents, Dave had a gnarly moustache, and I had long blonde hair. We were just two twenty-somethings hopped up on love and sunshine. We drank too much sangria on boat docks and sang country music too loudly around campfires. The proposal, the wedding, and the babies started to come up in conversation. They were something people romanticized. We had no idea what we were really walking into when deciding that we wanted all these things for our future.

We couldn't wait for everything we talked about – then we blinked, and it all happened. Dave became my husband. We bought a house. We had a baby – and then another – and then one more. We stopped drinking sangria, we stopped driving with our windows down, and we stopped staying up late snuggling by the campfire. The couple we were before had so much freedom. Loving each other, healing, laughing together, and finding time for one another came so easily. And the same thing rings true for me. Before kids, everything seemed to come easier, especially when it came to healing.

As a woman in the thick of marriage, kids, illness, bills, and life – I find it incredibly difficult to put time aside for myself for healing, whether it's from the overwhelming weight of my day-to-day responsibilities or navigating recent hardships that came with motherhood. Everyone's needs trump mine. But the truth is, pushing my needs aside only hinders what I can give my family. Especially my husband. Despite my best efforts, Dave sometimes feels like I've forgotten him. And sometimes, I can say I feel exactly the same. Marriage is hard. And being a couple that makes time for each other and trying to fill each other's needs while also being a parent may be one of the harder things about parenting. I'm hoping this is just a little kid thing – and when they can all wipe their butts, we'll find more time in our marriage to be with each other and not just parent together.

The world I'm raising babies in, the world I'm mothering in – is not always a kind world. It sure as hell isn't always fair. Everything we don't have is flaunted right in front of our faces through a little screen we control right in the palm of our hands. And all of it tells us we're not enough. It makes us feel like we should look more put together when our partner walks through the door. It sets the expectation that we should do a little nap-time hustle to help pay for the family vacation you desperately need. It guilts us into believing we should be having sex more, and dancing with our kids more, and laughing more, and simply being more. And the truth is, there is always room for improvement. I could be more for my husband. I could put more into my family. I could probably be a better mother for my kids – but not in the way we think we need to be.

Our society makes it seem as though it's selfish for a woman to fulfill her personal needs while being a mother. Then we see mothers break down, and we wonder why. We see marriages fail, and we wonder why. And it all comes back to pressure. It comes back to living inauthentically and then realizing it when you become a mother – a role with little time to dig yourself out of that hole. I couldn't dig myself out until I hit rock bottom. It took a lot of effort to heal and change my way of thinking.

5

UM, BALANCE IS BULLSHIT, RIGHT?

Many little girls grow up with the dream of being a
mommy. I was no exception. I spent my entire childhood
preparing for the role. I played house like it was a religion.
Heck, I even gave birth to a Cabbage Patch doll in my
bedroom. I thought I had it down, that I had mastered
the art of child-rearing. I expected that the hours I spent
rocking my baby dolls, along with natural instinct and
intuition, would make me the mother I had always dreamed
of being. The mom who fell into the role of motherhood
with simplicity and ease. The mom that baked cookies
and kept a clean house. The mom who never yelled and
was always available to her kids. I would be the mom who
would rock an adorable topknot while wrestling with my
babies on the floor. I was going to be *that* mom. But more
than anything – I wanted to be the mom I had growing up.
One that was involved, easy-going, and literally bursting
with love at every seam. I wanted to be a mom that I could
be proud of, that my children would be proud of.

Well, the jokes is on me. Heck, you may feel like you
had the wool pulled over your eyes, too. My introduction
to motherhood was M-E-S-S-Y. Like postpartum bleeding,

leaking nipples, crying with rage, black eyeliner running down my face while wearing the same pair of sweatpants three days in a row kind of messy. My body was messy. My relationship was messy. Friends, my hormones, and emotions – SUPER MESSY. Motherhood is messy. There was a lot of crying, a lot of cursing under my breath, and a lot of *what in the world did I get myself into?* For real, girls, *what did we get ourselves into?*

Motherhood has been hard for me – and I know I let it show much more than my own mother ever did. Maybe it's the result of coming from the millennial generation – I received a participation medal every now and then. But perhaps it's the result of the unattainable expectations placed on millennial mothers and women. I mean, really, could our standards be any higher? Being a mom seems more complicated these days than it was before, but it's always been a tough job. What's changed is the narrative around what a "mom" looks like. The pressure to be a great parent these days is fierce. In recent surveys, 80% of Millennial Moms said being "the perfect mom" is important. We all know there's no such thing, and yet we still strive for it. We expect ourselves to remain patient, consistent, calm, organized, healthy, and fun. And those are just the pressures we put on ourselves. We also deal with the anonymity that comes with a keyboard, where people can make comments to mothers that they would never make to their faces. But it goes beyond the pressures of competing with one another on social media.

Recent studies highlight the benefits of different parenting "styles" recent generations of parents are fixated on the proper ways to foster sleep, feed their children, discipline, and play to teach independence, build confidence, and promote self-worth. We try to be empathetic and open-minded in ways our parents weren't encouraged to be. But then older adults feel like children don't show the same respect they used to back in the day. We are in a constant battle with whether we're giving our children enough power over their independence or too much leniency, and we worry about the behavioural impacts all of our decisions have. With all of the information available to us, we're constantly questioning our methods and whether we're setting our children up for success. And to us, success means they are happy, healthy, and confident in their own body AND mind.

Millennial mothers were born in the eighties and nineties – the Spice Girl generation, if you will. Need I remind you of *girl power*? Our generation was raised by women who questioned the sexual division of labour in their households and the roles of gender in society. We are scrunchy-wearing-Tamagotchi-loving girls, and thanks to our foremothers, we grew up inspired. We fight the patriarchy, share our stories of survival, and combat continued exclusion with activism and democracy. Millennial women are aware, empowered, articulate, and high achieving.

At some point, all mothers from the millennial generation face a crossroads in their lives when we realize the equality dream isn't quite there yet. There is always something that needs to be sacrificed between womanhood and motherhood. It could be our job, it could be time at home with our children, it could be our relationships, heck, it could be our hair – I get ONE haircut a year, and I make it count with a mom-bob. When women become mothers, we suddenly feel as though we have to redefine who we are, and then we do it with less sleep and less clarity than we've ever had. At the same time, we're questioning if we could be doing everything better. We hold guilt over angering too quickly, not engaging our children the way we think we should, having unwashed dishes in the sink, and unfolded laundry in the dryer. We're attached to our phones, we're overwhelmed with information, and then we have costs – man, do we have costs. Daycare. Housing. Food. Gas. Insurance. Cars. Clothing. Formula (don't even get me started on the hypo-allergenic kind). And none of that money is ever spent on us, is it? You know that haircut I mentioned? There was a time or two I cut that damn thing myself. We're hemorrhaging money. Putting our kids in daycare costs nearly more than we receive in salary…but where do we find personal fulfillment if we leave our job?

Ugh. We're a generation of mothers unlike any generation before us, and we're stressed as fuck over it. We were empowered to be it all and do it all – but when it comes time to put that power to the test, we crumble – and I'll tell you why:

North America isn't built for the greater well-being of the family. It certainly isn't made for the well-being of the mom. Our generation lacks the village and support mothers before us once knew and valued. This isn't to say mothers haven't been struggling for centuries, because I promise you, mothers have been struggling for centuries, especially when it comes to equality, sexism, and little support from their partners. But mothers of today, we know a different struggle. We know the burden of being the mother, the wife, the friend, the employee, the sister, the daughter, and the very twenty-first-century concept: the side hustler. We know the burden of the work, life, and baby balance. We're expected to shower, smile, eat, stay fit, build an empire, maintain a clean home, maintain romance, maintain friendships, maintain our eyebrows (don't even get me started on my bikini line), raise a tiny army, run an envy-worthy Instagram page, and stay totally sane through it all. Nope. Not happening. And some moms are asked to do all this on their own, without the support of a partner, family,

something wrong. Perhaps I expect too
... this system isn't working for me. The
..... or hyping women up for most of their life and then
leaving them to raise the next generation with little support
or resources.

The scary thing is, when a woman enters motherhood,
she's not just battling everything that comes along with
being a MOM. She's also battling motherhood and
postpartum demons and all the emotional baggage and past
traumas she's never been encouraged to address. We have a
lot of grownup stuff weighing heavy on our hearts. There's
a lot of good stuff, too. A lot of good things happen. But
for some reason, it feels way easier to listen to the crappy
voice inside our head than the one that reminds us of the
good. Then we believe the crappy little voice inside of
our head, and it grows and gains power. It overcomes our
logical thinking. Just like my internal voice overcame my
logical thinking when kids made fun of me in the eighth
grade and when I stayed with my boyfriend because he had
my virginity.

Eventually, after all those years of negative self-talk,
we hit a breaking point. We lose who we truly are. Maybe
you were teased like I was when you were a young girl.
So, you change your hair or your clothes. Maybe your
parents pushed you into a specific post-secondary program
or career when you really had your heart set on something
else. But you finished the program, landed the big job,
and pushed down your true desires as you climbed the
corporate ladder and made the big bucks. Maybe you
stayed in that crappy relationship because you were
manipulated to believe you didn't deserve any better. And
through all these encounters, while molding yourself to

everyone's expectations, you lose sight of who you are genuinely supposed to be. Then your light burns out, and eventually, you enter this frantic state of self-discovery.

I've been on a frantic journey of self-discovery for what feels like ages. It started long before I even had babies. I can honestly say it started way back in the sixth grade when my family moved, and my world flipped upside down.

Kids teased me. They chased me home. Spit on my lunch. Called me horrible names and made fun of the way that I dressed.

It was something that changed the course of my life and pushed me to become the person who was always striving to meet everyone's expectations and fit a mold of what was "best," and "cool," and "right."

For a long time, there was a little girl in me who never had the opportunity to grow up. Someone else grew up in her place.

As I've been raising babies, I've also been tending to that abandoned little girl. But the influence of social media has made it so darn hard to connect with her. All I've ever done is compare myself to other women and mothers instead of bringing that little girl back to life.

Every blog I've written, every job I've taken, and every time I've said "yes" when it should have been a "no" has all had a bigger purpose. I believe that. Life isn't about having regrets. It's not about regretting all those times you have a half-ass "yes," but about growing from those moments, you didn't stay true to yourself.

This is your call to action to undo all those times you said "yes" and didn't mean with every ounce of your being. A call to action to release all of the people, places, and things that don't serve you to open up room for the things that truly matter. This is your opportunity to clear space for a bigger purpose as the universe sees fit.

You and me – we all have a purpose. And the longer we resist and try to meet an expectation that isn't true to our highest self, the longer it will take for us to get there. Some of us will never find our purpose at all because we're so consumed by everyone else's noise. There will be days where you're met with resistance, but those days are a moment to sit and realign.

You may have entered motherhood without the vulnerability that I had, or predisposition to depression that I had, or insecurities that I had. But I can almost guarantee that you entered motherhood with insecurities, bumps, and bruises. No one grows up unscathed by the people around them. And then there's all that millennial stuff we face as moms.

Despite our best ability to prepare and learn, motherhood sometimes leaves you blindsided – which is okay because motherhood IS blindsiding. But what we're not prepared for is the resurfacing of traumas and the clash we face with our inauthentic selves. So, we're left with an unbearable weight on our shoulders. Those uneasy feelings from your past resurface, striking you where you're most vulnerable.

To any mother feeling any ounce of doubt, this book was written specifically for you. I know you never expected it to be this hard, I certainly didn't. I don't think anyone does.

Maybe motherhood made you realize where you are in life isn't where you want to be – and that's okay. There is time! Being a mom doesn't mean life stops, it's a reason for your life to get started! My children are the reason I finally picked my butt off the floor. I couldn't keep living my life any other way.

If you're hurting or hustling or feeling pressure from both, you're not alone in this limbo. You are brave and strong, and your inner voice is putting pressure on you to make a change because it's time. It's time to stop living for everyone else and time to start living for yourself.

I know that sounds impossible when you have a kid or four that demands every ounce of you – but trust me, there really is no better time.

No one can walk through life gracefully with this much weight on their shoulders as a mother can. And I know you're thinking, grace? Me? HA! But you are, mama. You ARE graceful! You're getting up each and every day and raising babies while also trying to find that little girl inside of you that got lost along the way.

Motherhood isn't what makes you lose your identity. You lost it long before that. Motherhood just made it come to light.

While you may feel alone, scared, or unsure of what's to come, I can tell you one thing – you're not doing it alone. In fact, your authentic self is waiting for you on the other side.

Whether you're at a rock bottom like I once was, falling to the bottom, or starting at the top trying to avoid the bottom, relinquishing control and opening your heart to what's true is the first step to rediscovering you.

6

PAGING THE PERFECT MOTHER

There's a lot of 'stuff' that comes along with being a woman. Let's start with the obvious, our monthly friend, menstruation (or Aunt Flow, Cousin Dot – Shark Week…I really don't know where people come up with these names). But yes, our periods – the gateway to our fertility and the reason white pants are a no-no for three to ten days a month. You've had a visit or six hundred from Cousin Dot. Your uterus participates in Shark Week. You know the stages of the game – the before, the during, and the aftermath of your period. All of which come with their own set of quirks.

Then, there's all the 'stuff' that comes along with your period when you're trying to conceive. Many of us do this thing where we unintentionally become obsessed with our period when we're trying to have a baby. We get to know each stage of our cycle (and the texture and colour of our cervical mucus). We stock up on ovulation sticks and download the newest period tracking app. We become experts on the ins and outs of our cycle, all to narrow down that small twenty-four-hour window where we can get pregnant. Twenty-four hours. That's all we have. High school sex-ed made it seem a heck of a lot easier. For many of us, though, that's not the case. For many, conception can be a chapter that's confusing, frustrating, and filled with questions (that don't always have answers).

Next in the list of 'stuff,' there's a ridiculous expectation that women should be shaved from tip to camel toe. I'm not exactly sure who to thank for this, but I will give the nod to porn. Want to know why we spend six hours in the shower? It's because getting the hair out of every little nook and cranny takes time. Not to mention the time it takes to 'get ready' afterward – I have a forty-seven-step process that starts with a blow dryer and ends with a finishing powder

Other fun facts about being a woman? Our boobs clap when we run – even with a bra on. We can fit into a size four and a size ten all on the same shopping trip because of a little something called 'vanity sizing,' and let's not forget about sexual harassment, the glass ceiling, and the ridiculous standards porn sets for the way we should handle ourselves in the bedroom. Women are treated a heck of a lot differently than men. You know it, I know it, they know it. It's known. There's a double standard here when it comes to gender, and the list for women is exhaustive.

Women are shamed and discriminated against because we have a vagina. Not just today – but throughout history. Though, we have come a long way.

Ah, being a woman – and being a Millennial woman at that. Just so we're on the same page, Millennials, also known as Gen Y, Echo Boomers, and Digital Natives, were born from 1977 to 1995. However – because everything must be difficult – if you were born between 1977 and 1980, you're also considered a Cusper. Cusper's carry the characteristics of both Millennials and Gen X. Gen X is the cohort generation following the Baby Boomers but preceding the Millennials. Clear as mud? Cool.

The Cusperlennial Boomer-Y generation is a generation that is holding on for dear life. We have a coo-coo for cocoa pops housing market, a shaky economy, a competitive job market – a pandemic – heck, we're even trying to survive the term 'millennial.' Our generation has grown a pretty bad reputation for itself. Other generations love to trash talk about our ambitions, dreams, and goals, even our sense of style. And while nineties fashion is making a comeback (bless the high-waisted loose-fitting jean), I never understood why we went through a period of bedazzling our vayjayjays.

Anyway, Millennials. We're a generation that's drowning in school debt; we're trying to climb the corporate ladder with our "big egos" and sense of "entitlement," and then we have our mortgages, car payments, cell phone bills, groceries, and all the other whacky costs that come with being an adult. When it comes to living a relatively stress-free life, the odds seem to be stacked against us. This isn't to say that generations before us didn't have difficulties. Because man, some of the generations before us had it HARD.

I come from a line of European immigrants who made their way to Canada on a boat without two pennies to rub together. You read that right – without two pennies – literally, there were no pennies to rub together. They lived in a barn, worked multiple jobs (under terrible conditions), and made ends meet by eating beans and hot dogs while scrimping and saving every penny they earned.

Yet, studies have shown that our generation, the millennial generation, is the most stressed-out generation to date. We're also the most depressed group of mothers. All of us are sitting here waving our white flags for help – but no one is showing up. There is a mental health crisis among our generation, and I'm determined to discover why and find ways to help. This book is just one of the ways I hope to induce change.

I have weaved my way into every Facebook mommy group, drop-in class, and friend circle in my geographical area. And in talking authentically with other moms my age, I think I've found the secret sauce to our mental health woes – inescapable pressure.

While today's mothers have found more equality at work and home, many find it still isn't enough. Women today still bear the heavier burden over men when it comes to balancing work and family, despite changing views on how home and work responsibilities should be shared.

Then, throw in a pandemic – and my goodness, harsh realities are exposed. Not only when it comes to mothers but social inequalities. Lower-income and single-parent households got slammed during the pandemic, and every injustice they faced in a typical, pre-pandemic world was magnified.

During the COVID-19 pandemic, one in three women considered leaving their careers because of the pressure of literally balancing *it all*. Between caring for our children, running a makeshift homeschool, and keeping up with demands at work, women faced and still face extreme levels of burnout. Pre-pandemic, the pressures of life were still there. We just got a well-deserved break every once in a while if we were lucky. But during the pandemic? Any semblance of downtime happened in the only place we were allowed to be, within our own homes – which by week three of lockdown, we were sick-and-fucking tired of.

Mothers are the team's coach, quarterback (kicker, running back, and entire defense). We tend to our careers, manage our home life, find time to chase our dreams and ambitions and keep our finances in check. Should I go on? Mothers of today, millennial or not, are stretched so thin – and on top of that, we have a wonderful digital world of *perfect* mothers we're comparing ourselves to.

Ah, the perfect mother. The only type of mother many of us believe to be enough. The mom who cooks and cleans and showers and has – dare I say it – a 'side hustle' or a full-time job. The serene twenty-first-century mom. Perfect in every way. From the gap between her thighs to the limit on her Mastercard. We dream of being like her in nearly every way.

Until the evolution of the social media mama, I used to dream of being exactly like my mom, a woman of the baby-boomer generation. She gave up her career to raise her babies, and the woman executed her role flawlessly. It sure looked that way, at least. My life was literally *Leave it to Beaver* on speed (sprinkled with the perfect amount of Catholic guilt). The house was always clean. The laundry was always put away. My mom always showed us continued patience and love. She made it all seem so easy.

I'm one of the lucky ones to have a mother like her. Not every child has a *Leave it to Beaver* upbringing. For many, it's not even close. But I need to note this because my upbringing was a big part of why I wanted to be a mom. I wanted to live out the rest of my life as I did during my childhood – eating pasta sauce on Sunday, making pierogi at Christmas, and picking the perfect pumpkin every fall. I think all any mom wants to do is give their child a perfect, pure, and magical upbringing – but for me, I also didn't want the magic to end. Though, I had no idea just how *magical* things were about to become.

Squeaking just into the '80s (I was born in 1989), I grew up during a period of massive technological change. I still remember the day we received our internet via snail mail as a compact disc. It was dial-up, which means the internet traveled through our hard-wired phone lines into our giant (and heavy) desktop computers. This was probably sometime in the early-to-mid nineties. Though, my parents didn't bring the internet into our home until it was deemed essential for homework – which was around the eighth grade.

Even then, my parents restricted access to websites and messaging services. We were allowed on the internet for fifteen minutes at a time, which never gave me the opportunity to change my MSN messenger status to 'in the shower.'

The internet. It came, it grew, and eventually, it became a monster. In ten short years, I went from using MSN messenger to connect with friends to joining a platform called Facebook, which would truly change civilization *forever*. At first, it was a platform to keep up with friends and acquaintances from college, but the way it's evolved – I don't even think Zuck anticipated it.

Today, Facebook is a beast. There isn't any other way to put it. It's a photo-sharing, mommy-shaming, neighbourhood-watch social media site that draws billions of users worldwide. *Billions*.

With access to so many people, with so many different lifestyles, from so many walks of life, Facebook has become an unfiltered platform that, in many ways, showcases life in the most filtered ways. Social media moms can be spotted from a mile awhile, they have idyllic, colour-coordinated photos of their lives, their meals, their home, and their family on a perfectly curated feed. Where are the #reallife photos of bedrooms covered with plastic toys and dinner tables lined with take-out containers? Not every home is Montessori-approved, and not every mom has a beach house and bikini body. Thankfully, some new, keep-it-real Instamoms are popping up and gaining popularity (I'm talking about you, Libby Ward). And we need more of that. We need those Insta-moms keeping it real, raw, and honest.

After Facebook came Instagram, after Instagram came Snapchat, after Snapchat came TikTok, and by the time TikTok came to light, I was nearing my thirties and couldn't care to learn new technology, let alone a new app. With every new social media platform came new filters and ways to make your real-life look just a little bit better. A little cleaner. A little more envy-inducing little more of a highlight reel of the perfect and best parts of someone's life instead of the whole movie.

Becoming a mom during this decade of massive media growth showed me what mothering looks like outside the four walls of my home. Really, it showed me what mothering could look like in any and all circumstances, from my worst nightmare, like child illness or loss, to my furthest dreams – *seriously, how do some people have so much money?* My mom wasn't the only mother I could compare myself to anymore. In a swipe, I had access to other moms. Prettier moms. Wealthier moms. More successful moms. Swipe a little further, and there were influencer moms and celebrity moms. Moms were trending left, right, and center in their perfect homes, with their perfect bodies, while living their ideal life.

Then, there was me – with zero trend – sitting on my couch in a pair of pants I probably sneeze-peed in while rocking a greasy topknot, far from perfect.

My mom was never an influencer mom. We never wore matching outfits, she didn't have a signature topknot, and our house had some questionable paint colours (that would never fly on the 'gram), but she was and is everything to me. Yet, despite that, I grew increasingly anxious that I had to be both the influencer mom and the greatest version of my own mom. It wasn't enough. I didn't get my body back quickly enough, my house wasn't clean enough, I didn't cook enough, and I didn't have a career that was important enough – nothing about me as a woman or as a mother was enough. And so, the frantic mothering started.

7

PAT YOURSELF ON THE BACK FOR BEING STRONG AF

You picked up this book for a reason – only you know why. Since I'm not a mind reader, I can only tell you what I think: you picked up this book because you're looking for something *more*. Or maybe it was in a discounted bin by the checkout. There's no way to foresee my success, but I really hope you grabbed this off the bestseller shelf in hopes of living your best life.

The truth is, if you're looking for something *more,* you're not going to find it here. I don't believe in shaming, guilting, or even encouraging someone to be more than who they truly are. What you will find here, however, is the truth. My truth, the good, the bad, and the ugly. My truth about pregnancy, postpartum depression, and my experience as a woman in the twenty-first century. I may even dig into my reality around multi-level marketing (#sorrynotsorry). I promise I will also talk about the pros of that life.

Before my come-to-Jesus/ah-ha moment, I was frantically navigating my way through life. I was feeling lost and confused and obsessed with finding my place, just like many mothers are. It's not our fault, however. This idea that we need more isn't something we initially placed upon ourselves. It came to us over years of being shamed and redirected from who we truly are. Magazines at store checkout counters, peer pressure, media ads, news stories – all encourage more stuff, more happiness, more personality and charm, and beauty, More of that but less of who we are. You can be anyone you want but…no…not like that… Then, social media took the world by storm –a gift and a curse all wrapped up into one perfect little package.

The idea of more has weaved its way into our conscious mind through little snippets into everyone else's best moments…their highlight reel (which usually features some form of quinoa or chia seed parfait or cream-coloured backdrop). Through tiny squares and 150-characters, we've – intentionally or not – encouraged each other to strive for more in every aspect of our life.

Being more hasn't always placed mothers in such a frantic state of mind. But if there's a term to describe twenty-first-century moms, it's frantic – meaning wild or distraught with fear or chaotically conducting oneself. We're frantically extending ourselves beyond our capabilities and frantically pushing ourselves outside of a comfortable state of mind. And all of this frantic movement isn't to make us better mothers or, more importantly, the best version of ourselves. No, this frantic mindset is all because we're trying to keep up with each other.

I don't remember my parents being frantic when I was growing up—frantically packing lunches—frantically trying to find clean underwear, and frantically ushering us out the door to school. I don't remember a constant state of panic because someone was running late or someone couldn't find their favourite shirt, or someone forgot to change over the laundry. I don't remember growing up in chaos. Chaotic mornings and weekends. Chaotic buckling and unbuckling in a car littered with take-out bags, shoes, French fries, and sweaters. I don't remember stepping over random pieces of clothes, toys, or shoes to walk from one end of the house to another. I don't remember eating take-out unless it was for a special occasion. I don't remember my mom seeming so defeated.

I wish I could say that while I can't remember these things, there was still chaos, frantic moments, and messy parts of our home. You know what, I'm almost sure there were.

But it wasn't anything like this. Growing up, my life never felt frantic in the way it does as a mom. All I've ever wanted is to create a home for my kids—a place where they feel safe, comfortable, and loved. And I think I'm doing that. But man, our house is frantic. Our home is chaotic. Our house feels like it's in a constant state of disarray. And while I know I could blame myself, I feel like the issue runs deeper than that - because so many mothers struggle to keep their heads above water. Some of us are trying to give our kids the childhood we had and loved, while others are working to give their kids the childhood they never had.

I was a frantic mom. I was obsessed with finding balance. Compulsively pushing myself to be better – and it wasn't even all for the 'gram. It was to compete with it. If I cleaned my house, I wouldn't post it. In fact, I did just the opposite. Posting towers of books and blocks scattered all over my floors. I posted piles of laundry and piles of dishes. I even posted photos of myself taking my antidepressant medication. All in an attempt to normalize the parts of my life that felt hard. To show others that life wasn't always perfect. But it was a ploy, a cover-up. It was an honest look into the chaos of my home and raising young babies – but was it a look into my state of mind? Absolutely not. I wanted more.

It wasn't that I wanted more money or more vacations. Though, that sure would've been nice. I simply wanted the happiness everyone else seemed to have. I wanted the endurance they had. The motivation they had. The body they had. The sex they had. I wanted that feeling that there was more to me than the days I spent within the walls of my home raising children. I truly believed that besides being a mother, I was completely obsolete.

I laugh at that thought now. That I was obsolete. Back then, when I was frantic - when I looked in the mirror, I saw nothing but a ragged, worn-down mother looking back at me. There wasn't any independence there. I was hardly a person. I valued myself based on how much laundry I could put away and how often I could have a home-cooked meal on the table. I didn't love my body and the way it had physically grown, carried, and birthed a child. I didn't value the perinatal and postpartum traumas I had lived through. I didn't love any quality of who I was outside of being someone's mom. And even then, I didn't value myself as a person.

While I wasn't stuck in the past, the past was undoubtedly stuck with me. Every insecurity and every left turn when I should have gone right ill-prepared me for motherhood and the life it would thrust upon me. Every voice that shouted over my voice of reason caused me to stray from my path. I truly believe that if I had known I was Swiss cheese before becoming a mom and had taken the steps to piece myself back together again, I might have stood a bit more stable in motherhood. I can only begin to imagine what that would have looked like for me. The idea of feeling stable was so far out of reach – as a new mom, I was about as stable as a baby giraffe in nine-inch heels.

When I found out I was pregnant, I expected that I would adapt. Actually, that's a lie. At first, I thought: holy fucking shit, there's a baby in there – how is it going to come out? And then, I thought, no biggie – women do this all the time. I'll adapt. It's what we've always done. We adapt to situations – the good, the bad, and the hard. Mothers before us made it seem like they adapted so flawlessly to motherhood. It's why women keep having babies, right? Now I know we keep having babies because toddlers are assholes and baby pictures suck us back into a dreamier time. But before? I thought women did this because they felt fulfillment. I was so innocent and unaware.

While there are times in life when we are required to adapt, what is most important is finding our way back to our center. Especially in motherhood.

With all this being said, I have to remain truthful - motherhood is an absolute gong show – it changes you. There's just no other way to put it. It's messy. It's loud. It's chaotic. More than anything, it requires you to adapt constantly and quickly. You'll eat more macaroni and cheese than you even did as a kid, and you accept that things are just 'sticky.'

Motherhood. I can say it like it is – we're all moms here. We love those little munchkins to death – but I've never been mad when my kids go to sleep. Never. S*weet dreams, my love. Mommy needs some peace and quiet.* And then, 30 seconds later, we need to look at every photo we've taken of them since the day of their birth. *I miss you. I'm going to kiss you. Oh, fuck. I woke you up.*

When you become a mom – you change. Your boobs

hang lower, you become comfortable wiping someone else's snot with your own fingers – heck, you'll even watch poop force its way out of your baby's butt when they're constipated. No? Just me, then?

Motherhood causes you to adapt to living in a child-like universe. A world of mess and make-believe with our babies right at the center. But at the center of this universe, it should really be you. Now before you think, "Wait, your babies aren't the center of the universe?" I need to make something clear. They *are* my universe. They're just not at the center. I am. Because when a healthy mom isn't at the center holding the universe together, the universe gets gobbled up by a supermassive black hole.

As a mom who had three children in under four years – two of them wild, one sweet as heck, and none sleepers-motherhood has taken a lot out of me. My three beautiful babies are everything I've dreamed of. But I've still really struggled in my role as a mother. While being thrust into uncharted waters as a new mom, I was navigating prior traumas, massive insecurities, and postpartum depression. After maternity leave, I was returning to a career that did anything but set my soul on fire. Then, there was the tumor that threatened to paralyze a face I have always taken for granted. My father-in-law passed away. My friendships changed. Life happened. But the reality of having three babies stayed the same – I was a mother, so I suppressed all the hard things and focused on my children. Which truly was the worst thing I could have done for everyone. Eventually, it led to a mental breakdown, a difficult conversation with my family and my doctor, and a prescription for antidepressants.

My medication took on an important role, it was there to keep me rational. To keep the intrusive thoughts from encouraging me to walk away and end my life. However, there weren't any tools or conversations or mentorships to help me manage the expectations I set for myself or help me dig myself out of a hole that had been getting deeper for years. I truly felt like I was at it alone. There was so much I wanted to be for everyone, not to mention how much was demanded of me – so I put all my eggs in one basket and trusted my medication would get me by.

From there, I kept trying to "chase the dream" when in reality, I was already living it. I had a family, a loving marriage, and a home of my own, and if I had just stopped focusing on trying to make everything better, I could have realized that what I had was exactly what I needed at that moment in my life.

Look, as women, we can be anything we want to be. We can achieve anything we set our minds to. We're strong as fuck. But the key to being all you want is being reasonable about your expectations and pursuing them at a reasonable pace.

Pushing yourself beyond your limits or desperately trying to achieve perfection and success will only push you further away from happiness. And in a chaotic state of mind, your life will feel frantic. Not only will you be out of alignment, but everything else will be out of alignment around you, too. If you're anything like me, you'll turn to the 'gram and get sucked further down that hole of feeling like less instead of feeling like more.

For those who can relate – and I'm sure it's many, I know you're wondering how to pick yourself up from here. The truth is that it takes work and will require some self-discovery. What I can do is guide you through the steps I took to rebirth myself and grow into the alignment with the woman I am today, and in sharing my story, I hope you will find your own way.

8

PREGNANCY ISN'T ALWAYS #BLESSED

Before I even became pregnant with my firstborn, Jack, I was frantic about *becoming* pregnant. I understood that, given my PCOS, conceiving a baby could take time. From the moment I met my husband to when we started trying to have a baby, I became obsessed with my fertility. It needed to work.

To my shock and surprise, Dave and I were pregnant on our second cycle of trying. Which was our second month of marriage. This means the baby thing happened pretty damn fast, against our odds. It all seemed too good to be true for a girl who used to think with a doom's day mentality. And it was.

When I was expecting Jack, my social media accounts gave no indication that my pregnancy was a living hell… at least for the first few months. I shared adorable weekly bump dates and cute pictures of our nursery. Don't even get me started on the teeny tiny pants hanging in the closet. But there was a devastating and unknown truth behind each precious post and photo. Our world was falling apart.

When we hit the twelve-week mark, I felt like I could finally let go of holding my breath. From a medical point of view, twelve weeks is generally considered to be "safe." The risk of miscarriage goes way down. I followed the status quo and didn't say a peep about our baby until we hit that sweet spot. It was really fun hiding my pregnancy for that first trimester from work and friends. I would secretly sip virgin drinks after pulling a server discreetly off to the side. I called in sick to work multiple times with food poisoning while worrying whether or not I'd lose my job. I was a first-time mom with fears and weird twinges. Yeah, keeping it all to myself was a dream.

Whenever you want to share the news of your pregnancy is entirely up to you – but I think that: the earlier you share, the more people can support you. And most importantly, there will be more people you can call at midnight when you need a Reese's Peanut Butter Cup milkshake.

Just as promised, at our twelve-week ultrasound, everything seemed perfect. I can still see Dave's face beaming at the black and white screen. I can still feel what his hand felt like in mine. There it was – our baby. My dreams of becoming a mom were finally coming true.

The ultrasound tech printed off three photos for us to keep – which we immediately posted to Facebook. The caption read, "First comes love, then comes marriage, then comes baby. Wishes do come true. Baby Lawton coming August 2016". The likes started to roll in. The congratulations came in waves. It was real now. We were having a baby.

Little did we know, only days later, that my hand would be holding tightly to Dave's with tears running down my face and fear running through my heart. In the days following this ultrasound, we found ourselves anxiously seated in our doctor's office awaiting results we never anticipated to hear – that our baby had an abnormality.

I remember our doctor saying that our baby had a thickened nuchal translucency. It kind of sounds like a badass superpower. Maybe an extra chunk of fat? But what our baby really had was a soft marker for Downs Syndrome.

As quickly as the words left the tip of my doctor's tongue, the tears began to stream down my face. I could hardly catch my breath as I locked eyes with Dave. As my doctor recited the risks of our pregnancy, even she held back tears as she watched me fear for my unborn baby's life.

Remember those internet strangers I talked so fondly about? This is when I found them. In the hours and days that followed our doctor's appointment, I scoured the internet for similar results – for parents who had babies with a thickened nuchal translucency. Which, in fact, isn't a nuclear superpower but the amount of fluid behind the neck of the fetus. Thanks to the internet, I connected with many mothers who had been through the same type of finding. Dr. Google also presented me with all the potential side effects, downfalls, and worst-case scenarios.

Our generation is one of the first generations that can bring an ultrasound home and Google every medical term on it. This nifty little resource can be both a blessing and a curse…but mostly just a curse.

The other great thing about the internet is that it's a place where people go to share their horror stories. Someone ate spaghetti and coincidently lost their toe? You can bet your bottom dollar that there's a blog about it.

However, the internet can also be a place where people go to find support for things that aren't often talked about – bedroom fantasies, third nipples, whether pineapple belongs on pizza. The important stuff. It doesn't matter what rabbit hole you're going down, though, you're always going to find something that will keep you up at night (especially if you look at the pictures, don't even *look* at them). Want to know what to expect during labour? It's there. But click-bait articles and embedded links can also expose every single, worst-case scenario. Then, like any good murder mystery documentary, it gets hard to look away.

You must remember that the internet is unfiltered. There is access to unlimited advice and information. It's a messy mix of opinions and parenting philosophies. Much of it is conflicting, and only some of it is accurate. It's often accompanied by a bit of judgment. In previous generations, there were family and friends to guide you. To talk you through the ups and downs and help you figure out this parenting thing based on first-hand experience. Our village is primarily online for our generation, and sorting through it can place an unfair burden on parents.

During our testing, the internet, outside of social media, became a place I started to find the truth. It was the first place I learned that motherhood could be challenging, and it was the first place that I learned that pregnancy isn't always perfect. It was also one of the first places I turned to when I had a bad day or a round of bad news. No one in my immediate life would or could understand our hardship, so we hid it – until we couldn't hide it anymore.

It took a few weeks, but we finally got an appointment

with a high-risk team at our local children's hospital for testing and consultation. A Genetics Counselor prepared us for the worst possible outcomes. This included our child being born without the ability to eat, breathe, speak, or in the worst case, live. The word "termination" was thrown around more than I could stomach. At the moment, it all felt like a terrible, traumatic nightmare. I continued to imagine our baby. It's fingers and toes. It's heart. The shape of its perfectly round (and giant) head. The baby Dave and I created through love. A baby I loved without even meeting and would continue to love despite whomever they turned out to be.

After a grueling two weeks, we received a phone call that our baby's DNA testing was in. Once again, we found ourselves sitting anxiously in the chairs of a doctor's office with my hand gripping tightly onto Dave's.

First, we were told that our baby's DNA returned low risk for Trisomy 13, 18, and 21 (Patau syndrome, Edwards syndrome, and Downs syndrome). We also found out we would be parents to a baby boy. My heart literally exploded. I'm still picking up the pieces. Then, the other shoe dropped. A series of ultrasounds discovered that our son had a rare build-up of fluid between the 3rd and 4th ventricles in his brain. This raised concern that he may be at risk for something called a chromosomal microdeletion. *Was this for real? Was this actually happening to us?* We were healthy, we were young, and I gave up coffee, beer, sushi, and cold meats – how could this be true? We were faced with an incredibly tough decision. Our high-risk doctor recommended we go through with amniocentesis testing, with a 1 in 200 odd of a miscarriage.

Remember how I said my heart exploded when we found out we were having a boy? Well, after this news, I'm sure a piece of my heart died.

Our doctor explained that this procedure would provide a definitive and accurate diagnosis. She also explained that if our son had a condition that required special treatment at birth, our doctors would be prepared to save his life. At this point, we felt like we had no choice.

The night before the amnio test was truly one of the worst nights of my life. I lay in bed, sobbing into my pillow. The kind of sob with force, roaring up from the base of my stomach. Making me physically ill. I held onto my belly. I was asking my son to give me strength. Apologizing for what I was about to put him through—pleading with him not to die—telling him that no matter what, he was loved.

In the morning, Dave and I made our way to the hospital, saying only a few words to one another. When we arrived in our hospital wing, I was handed a gown and directed towards the changing room. I reluctantly undressed and placed the blue, cold gown over my belly and around my back. Continuing to question whether our decision to test our child in such an invasive manner was the right thing to do. Dave held my hand as we walked toward a hospital bed. Giving me a look of reassurance, reminding me that we were in this together.

Wires and monitors were attached to my tummy. Eventually, the ultrasound probe exposed our son, whom we named Jack, within the safe confines of my womb. There he swam. Happy, content, and in my eyes, absolutely perfect. I could hardly believe I was putting his life at risk knowing that despite the testing results, he was mine, and I would keep him.

As the needle was inserted into my belly, I could feel Jack's kick. I whispered to him, praying he would stay calm and still. Reassuring him that I would keep him safe. After the procedure ended without fail, Dave and I were advised that the results would take no more than three weeks.

During this time, to the world, I was pregnant and expecting my first baby. I was a first-time mom with a belly just itching to be rubbed. I should have been on cloud nine. Yet, whenever someone asked me if I was excited to be a mom – or even worse, when someone asked me how the pregnancy was going – I died inside. No one knew what we were going through, it was taboo to talk about. I wasn't walking around with a big note on my belly that read: *warning: asking this mother about her pregnancy will make her cry.* The ugly kind of cry.

We have to remember; that a picture is worth a thousand words – that doesn't just apply to pregnancy announcements or adorable baby photos. It applies to every damn photo-op we see on social media – vacation photos, engagements, a girl's night out (that you weren't invited to – ouch). There's a lot out there we don't know, and the photos we see have us thinking about where we fall short. But – just like marriage is more than a white dress and a black tuxedo, a vacation photo is more than just toes in the sand – it's the lost luggage, the food poisoning, and sometimes the drunk argument after a few too many all-inclusive mojitos. An engagement is more than just the ring – it's the wedding planning, spending an uncomfortable amount of money, and praying you make it to the altar. And a pregnancy announcement – it's more than just an ultrasound. There's a heck of a lot of fear that fills your soul when you find out you're going to become a parent – and then sometimes, there's more than that.

Our genetic testing was the first time I felt that I could be transparent about an imperfection. Not that my baby was imperfect because whatever the outcome, my baby would have been perfect to me. But answering questions with a false sense of hope or trying to hide that our son may be differently abled wasn't something I was ready to stand for. I didn't want him to try to meet a mold. I didn't want him to think who he was wasn't good enough (*hmm, yet I've never wanted the same for myself*). And truthfully, this was a situation we had no control over, and there was nothing we could do to change the outcome. Whatever it was that lit the fire under my ass to start talking about the hard has stayed with me since then. It could be because I want to set an example for my children so that they can be who they are without hesitation. That they can answer questions truthfully without fear of judgment. That they should stand proud of themselves, despite their circumstances. A piece of me also talks because I've come to find that people often don't talk enough when it comes to hard things. This is a shame because when I started to speak, I began to heal, and more importantly, I began to find people just like me.

Things are going to happen to us in life. We're not in control of everything – but (and I say this loosely because I know how hard it is to sit in the passenger seat of your own life with your hands off the wheel) we can try to find ways to manage our disappointments or anxieties, or sadness… but only once we've had the chance to accept them.

You can't celebrate the good or overcome the bad if you can't accept that it could happen to you in the first place. This was the first significant life circumstance I had to learn to accept – despite the outcome.

Our testing took eight weeks, not three, due to an issue with culturing – science, you nearly killed me. The phone call came in as I was sitting at my desk at work. The hospital's name popped up on my screen. It was 1:13 in the afternoon. You don't forget a call like that. I grabbed my phone and ran into the hallway, tucking myself into a corner where no one could see me cry. "Mrs. Lawton, this is Shirley from the Prenatal Diagnosis Clinic at McMaster Children's Hospital. I'm just calling to let you know that all of your test results have come back normal. Your baby is clear of any abnormalities." I collapsed to the floor and began to sob. The kind of sob with force, roaring up from the base of my stomach. Making me physically ill. I held onto my belly. My baby was going to be okay. I had no idea I wouldn't be.

9

THE BABY COMES OUT OF MY WHAT?

Do you remember those last few weeks of your pregnancy? What am I saying – of course, you do. People say you forget, but misery loves company. You do NOT forget. The final weeks (years) of pregnancy are long. Your body is hot, stretched, and sweaty. Your feet are seven sizes too big and swollen – and, if you're anything like me, your hormones are wild. With a larger belly and aches and pains, you'd think that *sex* would be the last thing on your mind during your third trimester – but nope, not for me. I needed the sex. Then, there's your man. Confused because he's wildly attracted to you…even with a baby in your belly, and also petrified he'll poke your baby in the face. I mean, come on, let's not be cocky.

Ah, the third trimester. Those three months feel like years. Then labour comes, and it's all over – and for some reason, we do it all over again.

We've outgrown the baby stage in my house, and it's become clear why parents have more children, usually two years after they have their first. *I'm going to try to be politically correct when I say this*…toddlers are "sweet little angels" who don't give a fuck. When they finally fall asleep after a day of setting the house on fire, we get sucked into the allure of a sweet, tiny baby who can't talk back and doesn't dump milk all over the floor. We'll do this one or two (sometimes three) more times and then finally learn our lesson that all babies grow up to be people – and to become people, they have to be toddlers first.

The check-out line at the grocery store seems to be the perfect place for elderly ladies to tell you how precious your babies are. They're drawn to new mothers like a moth to a flame. Imparting wisdom on unsuspecting mamas too overwhelmed to absorb anything but a gentle smile. They reach for the bare and tiny toes of infants. Squeeze the chubby and rosy cheeks of toddlers. And repeat similar reflections. "You're so blessed." "They're so precious at this age." "Isn't this phase so incredible?" "My kids are all grown up now, but I sure miss when they were that little." These encounters used to make me feel like crap. I'd smile – but inside, I was rolling my eyes. I'd think, oh yeah, you must have had it easy then. Your baby probably slept, latched perfectly right away, and hardly cried. That must have been the case, how else can you look back so fondly? And then I'd angrily pack up my groceries, wondering why the hell I didn't value the early years as much as everyone else.

I didn't get it. And then *insert stereotypical reflection* – I blinked. I had three kids, and my youngest is already two. The gummy smiles are over. We won't have any more first words, first steps, or first giggles. My baby chapter is done. And I get it now. I know why those ladies look at new moms with a sparkle in their eyes. They've learned that all the hard stuff is worth it. They know how fast it really goes.

One day, without warning, it all stops. One day you

won't have a baby, or a rambunctious toddler, or a curious preschooler to turn heads. One day, people won't stop you in your tracks to comment on your beautiful family. One day, your babies will be grown. And instead of throwing themselves out of a shopping cart or running wild down a grocery aisle, they'll be home on the couch or somewhere with their friends. Every once in a while, you'll manage to get your teenager out of the house and into a store… and when you're there, you'll blend into the background. You'll be just another family. You'll be the one stopping parents in their tracks to tell them they're blessed. I know you've promised yourself you won't do that – but you will. I'm already becoming the asshole who wants to grab onto a tired mom with a brand-new baby and tell her to hold on tight to the baby years.

One day, people will stop meeting your eyes with a kind and gentle smile. Your family won't pull on their deepest and most cherished memories as they reminisce about their good 'ole days. One day people are going to stop telling you that you're blessed. They won't tell you how precious time is and that it only gets better. Instead, like me, you'll turn your head and remember that just yesterday…you used to be them. How precious that little family is. The family with the squishy toes and cheeks. The parents pushing a stroller and a shopping cart, trying to keep those little bums in their seats. Extra toys and food are thrown in the cart, and big emotions draw the attention of those passing by. Those tired parents with dark circles and a look of defeat, you were just them yesterday. But gosh – you blinked.

One day this will all be behind you. And you'll know it because one day you'll look up and see nothing but people's backs…because nobody stopped to stare.

It's impossible to see it when you're in the moment, but

those baby years are some of the most extraordinary years of our lives – and they pass quickly. Time is precious. Especially when you're not actually in it. At the moment, it feels like a fucking eternity – but you blink, and those days are gone.

It feels like it was just yesterday when I went into labour with my firstborn. I spent six hours bouncing on my yoga ball, rubbing my nipples, and sucking back pineapple. I also spent the day making Scalini's Labour Inducing Eggplant Parm. Have you heard of it? Nearly three hundred baby pictures are proudly hung in Scalini's old-fashioned Italian restaurant in Cobb County, Georgia. All of those babies were born after their mothers ate the magical Scalini's eggplant parmigiana. This dish of breaded eggplant smothered in cheese, and thick marinara sauce claims to induce labor. Pffft, it was a no brainer. I needed the parm. At thirty-eight weeks pregnant, in the hot-hot heat of August, I sliced eggplant, layered mozzarella cheese, and threw my eighty-seven-pound casserole dish in the oven. I was desperate. It was the only way. My only hope was to get my baby out…seeing as my husband wanted nothing to do with poking our son in the forehead.

At around four in the afternoon that same day, when my nipples finally became chaffed from the twisting and turning, my husband walked in the door. He was just in time to play a game of, "is that my mucus plug in the toilet, or am I just happy to see you?" We couldn't decide. I did what any millennial would do and took a picture of it to send to my cousin, Carrie. It is what camera phones are for, after all. At the time, Carrie was one of the only people I knew who had a child – she should be able to help me figure out if the goopy stuff in the toilet was something to celebrate. After going back and forth over text about my symptoms and whether the goop was tinged with blood

– she determined: it was plausible. Meaning… the wait continued.

The dreaded wait for labour. A time when soon-to-be mothers frantically spot symptoms and reach out to their best friend and confidant, Dr. Google.

"What does a mucus plug look like?"

"Safe ways to naturally induce labour."

"Loose poops, am I in labour?"

"Flu-like symptoms, am I in labour?"

"Period cramps? Am I in labour?"

"My baby toe is itchy. Is that a sign? Am I in labour?"

LABBBBBBOUUURRRR.

I stuffed my face full of eggplant parm loaded with promises, and then followed up with an all-you-can-eat sushi buffet. Mama was hungry – and my near 8-pounder was running out of room. Afterward, we hopped in the car and drove over to a specialty computer store so Dave could pick up…*I couldn't tell you…it was something "computery."* Stepping out of the car, I felt a strange pop in my abdomen. "Well, it's finally happened," I thought, *"my bladder exploded."* I stood paralyzed before a buggy boy as my cervix transformed into Niagara Falls. He was no older than fifteen, and he was *traumatized.* The movie-worthy sac break. It only happens in 10% of pregnancies. And, of course, for me, it happened in public.

Before I go any further, there's something you should

know about Dave; bodily fluids make him anxious and uncomfortable (it's a wonder how we ever got pregnant). So, when my water broke – it sent him into a panic. He anxiously scampered around the car, throwing blankets on our cloth seats to protect them from amniotic fluid and other bits of baby juice. Remember: at this point, my cervix is still one of the seven wonders of the world. I'm going into labour. I'm worried about pooping on the delivery table. Dave and I are about to become parents, and I'm watching my husband have a damn near panic attack over some amniotic fluid on his precious cloth seats. With this all being said, in the last five years, he's had to catch vomit with his bare hands, and he's also been hit with flying poop – needless to say, he's come around. He hasn't really had a choice.

We made our way to the hospital, calling our family along the way. The baby was coming! Except, as we would find out – labour doesn't mean impending birth, so we were sent home to wait. Yeah. Apparently, if you're not contracting and you're not dilated, and the baby is as happy as a pig in shit, the best place to wait for the opening of your maternal cave is in the comfort of your own home. Which happens to be away from the drugs.

While labouring at home, it wasn't long before my contractions started to ramp up, and by that, I mean my uterus tried to kill me. I sat in our tub and not-so-kindly requested that Dave not touch me, not look at me…fuck, not be near me. Abiding by my rules, he left for the other room and built himself a brand-new computer. Have I mentioned Dave's an engineer? This means his social cues aren't always on point and techy things excite him. So, why wouldn't he build a computer from scratch after I banished him from my side?

It wasn't long until the pain became unbearable. With each contraction, my entire body tightened and clenched. But I sat in that bath for seven hours. I was breathing through the contractions every five minutes for a minute. The pain was unlike anything I had experienced before. It was like someone took a serrated knife, stabbed me in the top of my stomach, and slowly sawed down to my pubic bone. Whoever said childbirth is beautiful was surely full of shit. The contractions would stop for a few minutes and then start all over again. I breathed through them until I couldn't do it anymore. Crawling my way out of the bath, I told Dave it was time. He gathered our bags, put my arm in his, and walked me towards our car – we didn't make it until after I vomited all over our front lawn. Which Dave stopped to clean up – because, well, you know how he is with bodily fluids.

Despite the unknown of what was to come, that day was the first time in months that my anxiety about pregnancy, motherhood, and labour had withered, and all that remained was excitement. I felt fat, swollen, and tired. I was ready for our rollercoaster to be over; more than anything, I was ready to meet Jack.

~

The drive to the hospital was about six contractions long – approximately ten kilometers. I moaned and groaned and grabbed that "oh shit" handle every bump along the way. At the hospital, my charming husband – who became the fertile villain in my story by this point – ran to get a wheelchair while I stood in agony in the parking lot. Tiny bits of fluid dripped down my legs as I breathed through every contraction. Fun fact for those who never experienced it: when your water breaks, it doesn't stop breaking – with every contraction, you let out a little *squirt*. Good times, indeed.

The yellow hallway to the delivery ward was one I had walked before. I had become well acquainted with the yellow hallway through all the checkups, tests, and anxieties. There were stars on the walls donning babies' names and birthdays. There were arrows pointing visitors toward labour, delivery, and postpartum recovery wings. It was all familiar. Dave rolled me past the stars and the arrows as I cradled my belly. It was early in the morning, so I could see our reflection in the windows as he pushed me down the hall. And I remember imprinting that moment in my mind. The way we looked, just the two of us, together in that hall. We were youthful at that moment. Unaware of what truly lay ahead. It was almost as if we were leaving little bits of ourselves behind as we passed our reflection. I knew things were about to change.

After that day, there would never be just Dave and Annie again. The slow, quiet mornings, the long passionate evenings, the equally passionate arguments, and loud expressions of anger – those days would be long gone. Tucked away in a little compartment, never to be lived so vibrantly and youthful again – except through photographs and memories, and occasionally in a closet hiding from our kids. As we passed each window, I promised myself never to forget. I captured an image of just us two at that moment and ingrained it into my mind and heart. Because twenty-two hours later, we would become three.

Twenty-two hours. As many of you know, labour can take a while. For me, my first labour took twenty-two hours of harrowing pain, screaming, waiting, and praying for it to end. Twenty-two hours of horror, pushing, bleeding, tearing, maybe pooping, and definitely popping a hemorrhoid before a beautiful baby boy was finally placed upon my chest.

I remember my OB yelling, "Push mama, push!" – and gosh darn it, did I push. I bared down and called upon any and all Holy Spirits for strength as I watched my vagina's reflection in the mirror at the base of my bed. *Zero out of ten, do not recommend.* My baby's head was going in and out and in and out. My hemorrhoid was doing just the same.

My chin to my chest, knees to my shoulders, I pushed a little life into that world that, for Dave and me, would never be the same....and quite honestly, my body would never be the same either.

A nurse placed my beautiful baby boy on my chest, and all I could feel was instant relief...and some tugging as the gynecologist weaved stitches in and out of my vagina. Dave kissed my forehead as we both looked down at the tiny blue eyes looking back at us.

In the movies, when a mother meets her baby for the first time, it's always shown to be some sort of out-of-body experience. TV has painted a particular picture of the whole ordeal.

Let's start with labour – an exhausted and sweaty mother is screaming her way through the birth of her child, only to be glowing and perfectly groomed as soon as the infant is placed on her chest – completely beaming with adoration. Not to mention the baby's automatic latch while a room full of friends and family hang around watching only minutes after birth. *Hello everyone! I'm bleeding down there but come on in!*

TV can be full of crap sometimes. It can mislead you into believing something should look or feel a certain way. Especially when it comes to two very specific things...

okay, three specific things: romance, babies, and fancy homemade cakes. Mamas who have tried to make their kid a fancy fondant birthday cake know exactly what I mean.

Labour and delivery can make a mama feel foggy, disoriented, and even distressed. First, your baby is born – which is a marathon in itself. Then, the cord is cut, and your placenta magically wiggles its way out of your body. This is the best-case picture-perfect TV-worthy delivery scenario. Which many of them are not. Many births are traumatic and result in their own set of follow-up procedures. If mama and baby are both healthy, the mom gets a quick hello before the baby is cleaned, weighed, and wrapped – and then placed back on mama's chest for some skin-to-skin. *The golden hour.* Who the hell named it that?

This is the moment many new mothers expect to feel overcome with love. *Golden, if you will.* It's what the movies show us, anyway. However, movies are not reality. Not all mothers have that instant, overwhelming bond with their baby the second they lock eyes. Not all mothers even have the opportunity to hold their baby immediately after birth. When my second son, Maxwell, was born via cesarean, Dave was the first to hold him. Birth circumstances are unique to everyone.

The idea that love is instant and overwhelming places a harsh layer of guilt on a new mom if she doesn't experience a powerful first encounter between her and her baby. The truth is, there is no right or wrong way to feel after bringing a new life into the world. Some common emotions that aren't often talked about are: shock, exhaustion, and maybe even defeat. For me, after twenty-two hours of labour and over twenty-four hours without food – I was totally and completely starving. Not only was I hungry (and drained), but I was also in a state of shock at the reality that my son was in my arms. He was finally in a place which, at one time, I never expected him to be. I was also officially a mother. I gave birth. My body just performed something extraordinary. It was powerful.

Did I feel overcome with love as new mothers do in the movies? Certainly not. Looking back now, I feel immense love for that newborn baby boy. There is nothing that can compare. But at that moment, I was physically and emotionally exhausted from what my body had just been through. Wires were coming out of different parts of my body. My legs were numb from my epidural. I honestly had no idea what to expect recovery would be like… down there. I truthfully wouldn't have even known about postpartum bleeding if it wasn't for the book *What to Expect When You're Expecting*. When I finally got to the postpartum chapter, it was an absolute fucking shock. Imagine if I had never read the book at all?! Postpartum bleeding, postpartum contractions, postpartum hair loss, the POSTPARTUM POOP? Someone, please write a book on the entire postpartum experience and give THAT to a high school sex-ed class.

Outside of the minute-to-minute, hour-to-hour postpartum recovery circus, you also have the reason you're bleeding in the first place: a baby. A real live baby. I remember holding him for the first time, feeling completely overwhelmed. He was a lot more fragile than I had imagined – and tiny. He was almost eight whole pounds, but my goodness, was he small. I had never held a baby so fresh before, and honestly, I was afraid I would hurt him. I distinctly remember trying to get him comfortable when he let out a loud cry. I screamed for the nurse, asking for help because I thought I had broken his arm. I felt incredibly insecure and ashamed in those new and first moments of motherhood. I never anticipated insecurity was something I would feel so deeply, and I was overcome with the idea that everyone was watching my every move.

I was hardly in my mesh undies before my hospital room was filled with loved ones. Full disclosure, I invited them there – but they all arrived at the exact same time. Eight family members circled my bed and beamed at their first and only grandchild and nephew. The next chapter of everyone's lives sat in my trembling hands. As everyone illuminated at our picture-perfect family, I shifted in my bed. Clots of blood fell into my mesh underwear; my breasts swelled into my wireless bra.

While everyone I loved fussed over my baby, I excused myself to the bathroom with a shimmy off the side of the bed. I was starting to feel raw and sore. The fentanyl from the epidural was finally wearing off. The pain of the whole ordeal finally set in.

A human being had just come out of my body. My vagina was literally just sewn back up. I looked into the bathroom mirror – no longer glowing and pregnant but battered and bruised from birth. My face was swollen from an IV concoction of fluids and meds; I was almost unrecognizable –, and everyone was there. They just couldn't wait to meet the baby, and I felt obligated to let them. Would they have understood I needed time? Certainly, but I convinced myself otherwise. With a packed audience, I was in a state of vulnerability in one of the most life-changing moments of my life. As a woman, I wasn't confident enough to set boundaries. Something ingrained in me long before I became a mom.

It was an hour before everyone had left my room; by this point, my eyes were hardly open. All I wanted was to hold my baby. I pulled my baby up to my chest, slid my finger down his nose, and kissed the top of his head. Jack was finally here.

10

PRESSURE PUSHIN' DOWN ON ME

There's this ache I get when I see a new baby. It's not my ovaries – I know that ache. That ache leads to a human. And humans, my friends, humans are a lifelong commitment. No, this ache is different. This ache wants to scoop me up and throw me back in time. It wants to take me back to my most vulnerable state – the day I met Jack. I want to hold him again with the confidence I have now. I want to meet him again, knowing him the way I know him now. I want to experience seeing him for the first time through the eyes I see him with now. The love I feel for him now, with the understanding of time that I have now.

That same ache wants to take me back in time to one of those late, sleepless nights – just one…because there were a lot, and Lord knows I can't do that again. But I want to go back to one of those nights and hold him knowing what I know now. Rock him, knowing what I know now. Be still in the moment with him, knowing what I know now.

This ache even wants to take me back to the grocery store with little bums in the seat of the cart. And I want to walk around and show my babies off with the poise that I have now. I want to thank the onlookers with the self-assurance I have now. And acknowledge that yes, they are precious, and yes, time passes too fast – this I truly know now.

This ache, friends. It's overwhelming when I see a new baby. I just want to jump back in time, not forever, just for a moment, and soak in their babyhood with all the wisdom and strength that I have now. But I also know that my experience in early motherhood was all a part of my growth. I know the hard parts are all an important component of my story. I know that hindsight is 20/20.

Pregnancy with Jack – and with my other two babies – was literal torture. I hated being pregnant. My body didn't handle pregnancy well, both in the physical and emotional sense. Some women are radiant during pregnancy, but that wasn't me. I was basically a pregnant Grumpy Cat. I think I missed some sort of millennial training session that teaches you how to be graceful while creating a human. I certainly missed the session on how to pose flawlessly for maternity photos while wearing nothing but lace over my swollen belly. I also missed the session on selecting the best filter to use on the photo of my husband kissing my bump. My maternity photos were taken in my backyard while I was on bed rest, and I'm confident they're worthy of meme status. Oh, and when it comes to being graceful, pee was constantly leaking out of me, and I don't think I ever stopped crying.

Pregnancy was not my thing, friends. Without even getting into all my traumas and complications – the baseline for pregnancy was rough. When I was pregnant with my first child, I gained sixty-five pounds as I stress-ate my way through the unexpected. Ice cream wasn't my friend, and neither was stress. Then there was my irritable uterus which paired nicely with my irritable bowel and irritable personality. Not just in one pregnancy but all three. All and all, it was an irritably good time. In summary: pregnancy wasn't all sunshine and rainbows for me – and a lot of women can relate, maybe you can too. There are some seriously weird and conflicting emotions following that positive pregnancy test.

Now, as a veteran pregnant woman, I know the whole growing and birthing of a baby thing can be much more complicated than it seems. And motherhood? Remember chapter three? It's messy. I hate to be the one to reality-check everyone, but it won't be exactly what you imagined it to be. If you're a mom already, you know this. But if you're thinking of becoming a mom, all I can say is… (oh boy, I promised myself that I'd never give unsolicited advice…but here it is) even expecting the unexpected isn't enough.

At times, motherhood can be a storybook: bedtime stories, tickle fights, and whimsical seasonal holidays. Those moments are special, though hardly ever perfect. Someone always needs a snack/glass of water/poop after that bedtime story, and this can drag on for *hours* before your little crotch goblins are finally fast asleep. Then there are the other parts of motherhood. The parts of motherhood that are messy. These are the parts you'll feel trapped in, consumed by, and unprepared for.

For example, I learned I'm the kind of mom that hates the park. I hate the death-trap climbing structures. I hate the big kids (who are so much cooler than me) obnoxiously playing tag on the playground. I hate that the other moms bring better snacks than me and that my kids insist on stealing those snacks. Then there are all the places my kids can hide. And how I assume they've been kidnapped and begin to manically scream their name when I can't find them within three seconds. "Isn't that your kid right there?" *Yes, other mom. Thank you. The kid upside down in the bushes does belong to me.* There's also the jerk who doesn't pick up their dog's poop on the soccer field and the teenagers who leave their used cock socks by the swings. Oh, and don't even get me started on leaving the park. Holy guacamole. The leaving of the park. "Five-minute warning." "Okay, mommy! You're the best, mommy! I love you, mommy!"

Five minutes later

"Okay, munchkins! Time to go."

"NOOOOOOOO! NOOOOOOOO! THE PARK! AHHHHHHHHHHHHHHHHHHHHHH"

Mom lovingly picks up her child and puts them in the stroller as people look on like they're witnessing a kidnapping. *Should we call the police?* Suddenly, mom gets a kick to the vagina, and the kid drops to the floor like she's been stung by seventeen bees.

I. Hate. The. Park.

It's supposed to be this magical wonderland of summer memories. The place where I'm supposed to meet up with mom friends and sip coffee while my kids run playfully through a luscious field of green grass. Instead, my eyeballs are darting in six thousand directions, trying to keep tabs on each of my kids and all of the ways they can break a limb. And the only "mom friend" I've connected with is the one who rescued my kid after he flipped upside down in a swing while I was trying to stop his brother from peeing in an open field. The park is not for me, folks. Nuh-uh. I hate it. Do you know what I love, though? The fact I've become so crotchety. Motherhood has really made me blossom into someone wonderful. Motherhood, my friends, is messy. You won't be the mom you expected yourself to be.

Your house will be covered in yoghurt and a light dusting of goldfish crackers. You'll scatter Cheerios like chicken feed for breakfast at some point or another. And you know how Cinderella's magic carriage turns into a pumpkin? Well, one day, your cute little two-door coupe will turn into a van, and it'll basically be a traveling garbage can—McDonald's French fries and Tim Horton's cups everywhere.

Motherhood is messy. You can't have nice things. And if you do have nice things, expect there to be boogers on them. The role isn't always glamorous. Hardly. Though adorable pregnancy announcements, gorgeous maternity photos, and staged family photoshoots make it look like it is. Behind the unicorn-embezzled onesies and those pregnant bellies covered in lace, there are the emotional messes that mothers face. The kind of messes that leave you packing a go-bag for Mexico.

No one really talks about these messes, though. Well, I guess they kind of do. Pregnant women receive all sorts of helpful advice, "Sleep when the baby sleeps," "Enjoy your sleep while you can," "Sleep. Find time to fucking sleep." And now, it all makes sense why.

The exhaustion you feel after bringing your first baby home is unlike any kind of tiredness you've ever experienced before. It's the kind of tired where you'll find yourself putting the milk away in the microwave instead of the fridge. And why is that? Why are we so exhausted? Well, for one: we're up 600 times a night trying to feed a little creature we just met (and created). The first few nights aren't all that bad, you're running on adrenaline and fresh baby smell – which is uterus, folks. That new baby smell is uterus. (Think about that the next time you take a whiff of somebody else's newborn baby). Slowly but surely, your cute little baby loses its allure (and its smell), and you want nothing more than a peaceful night's sleep. You're just happy to see them in the morning – the cute will still be there.

Baby has other plans, however. Baby is hungry, the baby is growing, the baby is going to scream their head off until you stick something milky and delicious in their mouth. So, you get up each of those 600 times a night, and you try to feed them. But the feeding thing doesn't come easy, and your baby screams. And screams. And screams. Eventually, Dad rolls out to the couch because he has to work in the morning and mama sits all alone trying to get this damn baby to eat.

Nights go by like this. Weeks even. The boob can't seem to do its job. Or maybe it does, and your baby can't figure out how to suck or fart, or burp. So, you make an appointment with a lactation consultant, and they tell you not to give up. They touch your breasts and mangle them into your baby's mouth. The pep talk is supposed to be empowering; instead, you feel vulnerable and exposed. Trying to do something that's supposed to be easy and beautiful, but it's actually dark and painful and frustrating.

That's how breastfeeding felt for me, at least – dark and painful and frustrating. It simply didn't work. My baby wasn't able to latch. Not a bit. Not a chance. And what do moms do when they can't get their baby to latch? Let's all say it together: they blame themselves. And why do we blame ourselves? Because it's pushed down our throat that breastfeeding is natural and easy and, most importantly, best.

In an effort to be prepared, I met with a lactation consultant before I had my baby. Yep, call it like it is – I was frantic about breastfeeding. I wanted to know *everything*, like the best tricks to get my baby to latch, how to hold him when he was nursing, whether I needed a breast pump if I should bring bottles to the hospital – *a*nd I wanted to have a plan if it didn't work out. Ah, a plan.

Quick fact: when it comes to parenting, almost nothing goes to plan. But despite that, the lactation consultant confidently provided me with a plan – and it was not to give up. It was super wise advice from someone who would swoop in and feed my baby while I was having a nervous breakdown at one in the morning, right? Except, there wasn't anyone to dive in and feed my baby when breastfeeding didn't work. There was only me and my husband and my husband's useless tits. I was even told by my friend, the lactation consultant – get this – not to have formula at home because it would be *too easy* to give my baby a bottle.

Oh, friends. I'm in three kids now, and boy, do I have a lot to say about that crappy advice. First and foremost – and most importantly – what kind of fuckery is that? Don't have formula on hand because it's *too easy* to give your baby a bottle. WHAT IF MY BABY NEEDS A BOTTLE? And not just that – what if I NEED to give my baby a bottle for the sake of my MENTAL HEALTH? Because friends, my mental health tanked even further when my baby couldn't latch. Suddenly I had to provide enough nutrients to keep my baby alive using only my body, and I couldn't get it right. It drove me crazy. I'd flip from son from breast to breast with growing frustration and impatience. He was only a few days old, and I was already resentful. *What kind of mother feels this way?* And yet, it wasn't either of our faults. My baby was trying. He did his best – it was all new to him, too! My breasts were even LOADED with milk, simply overflowing. Engorged. Swollen. I was an over-producer. What did I have to be upset about? Mastitis was creeping in the shadows, waiting for the perfect opportunity to kick me when I was down (which it did). Breastfeeding just didn't work out. Not for us.

A poor latch isn't the only reason a baby may not be able to feed. Some mamas have a baby that will latch but aren't as fortunate to have a quick and plentiful milk supply at no fault of their own. Even more so, some mothers may feel uncomfortable breastfeeding. It could be due to past trauma or possibly due to a nursing aversion (which is actually very common). And yet, they still feel pressure.

Ah, yes. The pressure. Did I mention that women live under a lot of pressure? We're pressured to fit in, to be popular, to be skinny, to be the do-it-all-mom, and yes, we're even pressured to breastfeed. Not encouraged, not supported – pressured. The saddest part? After being bombarded with pressure our entire lives, women become accustomed to it. Instead of growing confident and comfortable standing up against the pressure no, we grow accustomed to giving in to it. We lose our voice along the way. And in motherhood, there is nothing we need more than our voice. Not because we need to advocate for our children. When it comes to advocating for our kids, no one can quiet the voice of a roaring mama bear. But when it comes to advocating for ourselves? We go mute.

I have met so many mothers who experienced the pressure to breastfeed. I also know a ton of mothers who had an easy and wonderful breastfeeding experience. And every feeling is valid whether you loved or loathed breastfeeding – or even if you felt meh about the whole thing.

I've experienced every emotion under the sun when it comes to breastfeeding my babies. For my first, I loathed it. My second, *meh.* And my third, I'm18 months into nursing my baby girl, and I secretly adore every minute of it. I think it's because it came so easily after two hellish nursing experiences.

It has been a different experience for each baby because – get this – every baby is different! And what works for one may not work for another, and so on. This mantra applies to every aspect of parenting. Some babies sleep through the night; some don't. Some babies nap well, and some don't nap ever (another beautiful trait of my firstborn). Some kids are stubborn, curious, and strong-headed; others go with the flow and eat all their vegetables. Say it with me: "every child is different." This is why, at the end of the day, you need to do what works for you and your baby. Yes, the experts have their place in the whole parenting picture. But we're also gifted with something really special, and that's our intuition. It's been there our entire lives. It's the little voice that has told us not to trust a certain friend, or to leave a relationship, or whispers, "I don't care what's in style, I like the way this shirt looks on me." THAT VOICE. The voice we've pushed deep, deep down inside. It comes ALIVE when we become a mother. That's what makes all of this so hard – we are finally forced to face ourselves in light of what everyone else has projected on us. And then, we have a big decision to make. Do we listen to the little voice inside? Or do we continue to fight it to fit someone else's mold?

Many first-time moms start this journey trying to meet someone else's expectations because we don't know what's coming. You never know who you'll meet on the other side of that umbilical cord. But as we become more confident in our parenting – which takes time and experience – we slowly start to do things our way. The problem is, by then, the damage has already been done. And it happens when we're most vulnerable. When we're new to the game.

Three kids in, I can confidently tell Tom, Dick, and Henrietta to fly a kite when it comes to my parenting. But as a first-time mom? All I did was try to comply, comply, comply. Starting with the world of breastfeeding.

After breastfeeding didn't work out, I decided to do the "next best thing" – exclusively pump aka, use a nifty little machine to express milk from my boob and then feed my baby breastmilk with a bottle. Which, let me say, is one of the hardest things I've done as a mom. And I had a baby during a pandemic. I'm only five years into parenting, and people say the worst is still yet to come (thanks for those uplifting pep talks, by the way), but pumping was hard fucking work. I'd rather deal with a daily diaper blowout. Give me the messiest blowout you got. Every day for the rest of my life. I'll take that over doing the whole pumping thing again.

For weeks I mangled my breasts into the shape of a hamburger, shoving them into Jack's mouth and failing at every attempt. At each and every feed, you would find both of us crying, me sweating, and my husband standing by with his useless ta-tas, watching it all go down. It finally got to a point where we decided enough was enough. We wanted our son to have the best (as per the *experts), but breast milk in a bottle would suffice for us*. It was then and only then that I resorted to a bottle at the hands of my double pump. The formula was evil. The formula was a big no. Formula meant failure. *Those experts really know how to hype a mother up, don't they?* Another sidebar, as I call bullshit. Lactation consultants, I really do want to begin by saying I respect you. Not all of you are so pushy; I'll give you that. But my experience was poo-poo, so here's my public rebuttal:

I spent hours attached to my pump. Hours. Thankfully, it didn't hurt. My husband would find me sprawled on the bed, milking myself like a cow at all hours of the day and night. It reached a point where I fully anticipated I'd begin to moo beyond my control any time I revved that bad boy up. *Moo-freaking-moo.* I schlepped my equipment everywhere, from home to my in-laws and a romantic weekend away for my first wedding anniversary. I even pumped while riding a shotgun on a summer drive down the highway. I was milking myself as my pump sang in unison with the radio. Waving to strangers as they drove by while my nipples stretched in and out of a contraption they'd never seen before. Poor buggers. A pump in action can totally ruin the allure of boobs.

Then there were my hands. Oh, my poor hands. My hands started to turn raw from cleaning bottles and pump parts every hour on the hour. Some little nooks and crannies can only be reached with special brushes. Everything must be sterilized to be safe. There was a process – and it literally came to a point where I was doing it with my eyes closed because I couldn't keep them open. I grew resentful of myself, and of my baby and the whole damn experience – for that, I had failed again.

This entire process went on for six months. Pump, feed, clean, repeat. Pump, feed, clean, repeat. Daytime, nighttime, anytime. Our kitchen counters were littered with fancy drying racks, and our freezer was full of whatever leftover milk I could scrounge up. My spirit was deflating with each suction of the pump. Eventually, my milk production started to decline, and I had no choice but to supplement with formula. *The dreaded, no-good formula.*

It took a lot of convincing for me to mix that first bottle of formula. I honestly expected my son to have some sort of freak allergic reaction. I was terrified that the little bottle of formula would kill him. I hesitantly boiled the water, measured the powder, and mixed his first bottle. Then with a deep breath and a prayer, I put it in my baby's mouth and started to sob. I was nothing but a failure. This was not the way it was supposed to be. This way of feeding was not *the best.* (Full disclosure, I believe fed is best – whichever way you choose to feed, so come at me).

Everything I read told me not to give up on breastfeeding. The books, the blogs, and even the pamphlets from the doctor's office. Don't give up on nursing, don't give up on schedules, don't hold your baby too long, and don't rock them to sleep. Try baby-led weaning/don't try baby-led weaning. Cry-it-out/don't cry it out. My mom gave me different advice from my pediatrician, my pediatrician gave different advice from my therapist. It was all a mishmash of information, and I felt lost. What was the right thing to do? How do I raise a happy baby who sleeps and eats, knows his A-B-Cs, and can work a tablet by age one? *Or am I not supposed to give my kid a tablet?* How am I supposed to survive these years? How do I survive at all?

There was only one way for me – I had to find my voice. I had to grow my confidence not only as a mother but as Annie. I had to peel back the layers, uncover all my insecurities, and identify what truly felt *right.* I had to create a stage for my intuitive thoughts to speak to me. I had to understand that less was truly more.

11

YOU GUYS...I THINK I'M LOSING IT

Bringing your baby home for the first time is kind of like your first week at college. You're excited, you're nervous, and uncertain. You're starting a vast and new chapter of your life, and you're trying your darndest to take it all in. Except it's all a complete blur. You drink too much Tequila; your clothes fall off; you walk around discombobulated from all-night bangers. Yeah, new parenthood is just like that. Except instead of tequila, you're drinking coffee. But you're still walking around with your nipples out, completely discombobulated just the same.

Your house isn't a humble little abode anymore – it's a frat house. Bottles and pieces of clothing scattered about, a light white dusting of powder on your bedside table – it's formula, folks, let's not get ahead of ourselves. There are boxes of cold pizza tossed upon your dining room table, old makeup streaked across your face, and a weird smell from the trash can. Babies are can't walk or talk back, and yet, they put everything in disarray. New parents are overcome with animalistic pride. So, when people want to meet our cubs, we welcome them into the jungle despite the chaos.

My life was just like that after bringing Jack home – and it hasn't returned to a state of harmony since. My house is always messy, pizza boxes are always lying around, and a pot of coffee is always brewing.

Friends and loved ones couldn't wait to swoon over the generic combination of Dave and me. Our little blue-eyed, blonde-haired Jack Josef. Acquaintances came, too. People I hadn't seen in years came out of the woodwork. It was like having a baby was an exclusive club, and everyone wanted a membership pass.

At first, we welcomed the attention and let everyone in. It didn't matter if we were running on three minutes of sleep or if it was closing in on feeding time, visitors came when it was convenient for them. And not only did they come when it was suitable for them, but some of them even came late. Rude. You all, if I could rewrite the definition of rude, that would be it.

Rude

/rōod/

adjective

Visiting someone with a new baby AND SHOWING UP LATE.
(Did you come without a prepared meal, too? See definition for an "ass").

Every new parent has had one of those people stop by. So, if you're one of those people who is *always* running late, send an Uber Eats gift card instead. That new mom is planning feeds and nap times around your visit, and if you arrive five minutes too early or stay five minutes too late, you'll muck up the entire system.

Our house was a local tourist attraction for weeks after Jack was born; of course, he was the headline show. I quickly began to feel invisible. One minute, I was an adorable pregnant woman at the center of everyone's world; the next, I was a tiny, unremarkable particle out in the universe. Now, I was just Jack's mom. The boob. The one he got passed back to when he started to fuss or get smelly. Everyone else's prize was here, and I was just the consolation.

Between visits, I navigated the world of new motherhood. Which usually meant sitting on my couch while staring at my baby in complete and utter shock. Was this real? Sometimes, if I was lucky, I'd manage to eat a piece of toast before brewing a pot of coffee, throwing our laundry into a closet, and welcoming another set of guests into our home. It went on like this for weeks.

The chit-chat was always the same. We'd recap my labour and then talk about whether or not Jack was a good sleeper. At three days old, what kind of fucking question is that? Especially from visitors who have kids of their own! Then, as soon as our visitors sniffed him enough, they'd leave – and we'd fall onto our couch into the unknown.

Between all of the visits, I was running around to endless appointments for my new baby. He was poked and prodded. Lactation consultants tried to help me with his latch, our pediatrician checked his weight regularly, and an audiologist checked his hearing. All to ensure our sweet little Jack met his milestones and got everything he needed. But was I getting everything I needed? Certainly not. Not even close. I wasn't eating enough, sleeping enough, or drinking enough water. And those are just the bare necessities to stay alive.

I was lucky to have a family practitioner who really cared about my well-being, which I've learned isn't always the case, especially for moms in the U.S who receive minimal postpartum care. At the end of every baby well-check, she always looked lovingly into my eyes and asked, "And how are you?". She knew I wasn't okay, and I could see her trying to wedge her way in. "Oh, you know," I'd giggle. "I'm tired but isn't everyone?" Hardy-har-har. She'd find some reason to book an appointment the following week. I knew it was never for the baby – she kept me close for when I needed her while respecting my boundaries and my process. My process was something that was going to take time – I'm just grateful Dr. MacEwan was standing close by.

In every prenatal class and parenting book, I knew what I was supposed to do with my baby. I knew how to change him, burp him, take his temperature, and run his bath. I knew *too* much, thanks to Dr. Google. But there was nothing to tell me how the hell I was supposed to take care of *myself.*

Those first weeks home, I was engorged and bleeding, and my second-degree tear was sore and stitched up. There was no immediate appointment or follow-up with my OBGYN. The hospital sent me home with some painkillers and stool softeners. *Have a happy poop!* I felt like I was thrown into motherhood with the expectation that my instincts would kick in. There's no immediate plan in place to follow up with new mothers. Which, to this day, seems bizarre to me. I guess that's not totally true. There are midwives and doulas. And anytime I've shared my disappointment regarding postpartum care, there's always a group who shames me for not setting myself up with a midwife. Fun fact: when you have a high-risk pregnancy, you're not eligible for a midwife. And if you want extra support, it costs money out of your own pocket. Moral of the story: postpartum support beyond the doctor's office is a privilege.

Everyone seemed confident in me, so I mirrored their expectations and appeared confident in myself. But I quickly learned I was a mess, and it wasn't even in the most obvious ways. I didn't cry or rage or even struggle to get out of bed in the morning. My son was my light. However, I've never judged myself as harshly as I did in those early days. Only one thing went through my mind: if there were instincts in motherhood, I didn't have them.

I didn't know how to handle colic or late-night feedings. Breastfeeding sure didn't come as nature intended. Every cough, runny nose, and fever sent me into a panic. I was an anxious, over-analytical mess. My instinct didn't help me learn how to live in my new and very foreign body. It didn't make me feel any less hideous as I stood in front of the mirror facing a girl I hardly recognized. It didn't make me feel confident as I paraded around my husband with twenty-extra pounds on my hips. It didn't make me feel comfortable sharing my intrusive thoughts with those closest to me.

Do you know what instinct did come to light, though? My need to frantically hyper-fixate my attention on something else. That quirky little voice in my head roared, trying to direct me away from feelings of failure, away from the things that I couldn't control. I had this unshakeable feeling that I was less than my son deserved. That I was lacking something, all the other mothers had. So, I decided I had to work harder on being the best damn mom I could be. I was so vulnerable back then. Frantically trying to be the picture-perfect wife and mother. Scrambling every morning to make it to our mommy and me class when I had barely slept enough to drive safely. I was supposed to be out there with him. Singing songs and supporting his development. Then, I was supposed to come home and clean my house. Make a home-cooked meal. Play patty-cake and read books. I was supposed to smile when my husband walked in the door. But I didn't have it in me. While I was so grateful to be spending time with my son, there was something missing at the end of the day – a sense of fulfillment. Motherhood was supposed to give me that. Everyone said it would.

Here's the truth about fulfillment in motherhood – there will be moments that will fulfill you, and there will be milestones that will fulfill you, but motherhood alone will not fulfill you. It's like how people believe money can buy happiness. Money can't buy everything, especially happiness. Health, family, and friends (the good kind) can't be bought. And kids, well, they don't just come into your life and flick on some fulfillment switch. They're not meant to fill a void. If anything, children draw attention to the voids in your life. What's especially challenging about that is that sometimes those voids aren't exactly straightforward. Understanding your voids takes time and self-reflection. It's an introspective process. So, where do we place the blame? Motherhood. For those of us who feel like we were destined to be maternal, the lack of fulfillment is a heavy blow. *You mean the fulfillment isn't instant?* It's not. Fulfillment ebbs and flows in life, and you're not going to find it in one place – especially not in motherhood.

When I realized motherhood didn't make me feel instantly fulfilled – as the world promised me – I began to think I was broken. But instead of hiding in a bathroom stall as I did as a kid, I began to seek refuge in my closet. A safe, dark space where no one could see me for who I truly was – a failure.

I could hear voices inside of my head telling me I was unworthy. It felt like a note was being passed around my inner circle – *Annie isn't feeling fulfilled* – and eventually, I'd be the butt of the joke. Once again, I was the girl who couldn't meet expectations. The girl who wasn't quite there yet. The girl no one could love or like.

I projected that pain onto Dave. Pushing him away as I navigated early motherhood with shame. He was dealing with his own set of emotions that come along with being a new father. After a day's work in a sleep-deprived haze, he'd come home to relieve his equally sleep-deprived wife. There was pressure to be the breadwinner, along with being a new father. He needed downtime to recharge and wrestled with guilt as he figured out how to navigate cycles of emotional exhaustion and guilt. All while figuring out that you *always* have to tuck a baby's penis down into his diaper to prevent leaks and slowly watching his wife slip away.

My man – the guy who vowed to love me till death do us part – wasn't equipped to manage my resistance to motherhood. While I felt unprepared for motherhood, Dave felt like no one had prepared him to support me. When he tried to present the idea that I was battling postpartum depression, I met him with rage. Who the hell was he to tell me I was depressed? I physically carried the baby. I went through labour. I couldn't breastfeed. I…I…I. There was a divide between us. No one prepared us for a divide and a resentment that crept into my headspace despite my best efforts to keep it under wraps. I felt utterly alone.

As a new mother, I'd watch my husband leave for work in the mornings with his laptop bag thrown over his shoulder and lunch tucked under his arm. The door would close, and I would be alone. By the time he'd arrive at work, I would only be taking my first sip of coffee as I pulled a baby out of a highchair and began to scrub sticky fingers off of every surface. With a few blocks for him to play with on the floor, I'd place the baby down and quickly eat leftover scraps from the plates scattered on the counter. While my husband was at work challenging himself, climbing the corporate ladder, and engaging with adults, I was at home, usually unshowered, wrestling kids into clothes, coaxing kids into naps and sitting with someone on my lap while I peed.

When we first got married, Dave used to come home to a different girl than he does today. She was sassy and fun. She wore a little rouge and a sexy bra. In those early days of motherhood, he'd come home to find a girl with spit up on her shirt and unwashed hair. A girl with a lame attitude and not a whole lot to say about anything but poop. She was a girl who didn't look like she was trying. But my goodness, she has been trying all damn day. From the minute she rolled her tired butt out of bed to the minute she crawled back in it, she had been trying. She tried to wash her hair, change her clothes, and make herself something to eat besides toast. She spent half the day running around with two kids wrapped around her legs and the other half down on the floor, racing little toy cars and humming the tune to Baby Shark. In those early days, that girl was spent.

It became so hard to relate to life outside of the home. I quickly forgot what it felt like to be anything other than a mom. You must understand that I am so grateful for the time I had at home raising my babies. But gosh, I really believe if paternity leave coincided with maternity leave or if there were more opportunities for support – my experience would have been different. Happier. Maybe even more fulfilling.

While I grew up in a loving home, with a loving family, and the *Leave it to Beaver* childhood, I still wasn't set up to succeed as a mother – because I believed motherhood was supposed to make me whole.

Every time I pivoted who I truly was to fit into a place I never really belonged, I lost a part of myself. And it all started when I was thirteen. It was the age I first realized that I wasn't someone people wanted to be around. It was the first time I changed who I was to be someone I was never meant to be. When I finally got to motherhood, I was already broken. If I could compare myself to anything, it would be a piece of Swiss cheese. The foundation was there, but there were some holes.

No one ever really said it to me, but motherhood is meant to be hard. There is whining and tantrums, messes and crankiness, sleep deprivation, and poopsplosions. And those are just the "small people, small problems" side of things. Big kids come with their own chaos, too. Which I can't even begin to think about. Re-connect with me in ten years, and then we'll talk. You won't be perfect. Motherhood is meant to come with some sort of identity crisis. It's not supposed to be easy peasy lemon squeezy… it's also not supposed to break you.

My half-ass identity, my previous battles with depression, and my high-risk pregnancy didn't give me a chance to embrace motherhood. Within the first two weeks of having Jack home, I developed a fear inside of me that ate away at my heart, my soul, and my optimism. I wasn't enough. Yet, I kept this fear to myself. No one could know. And even more so, who could I tell?

My gynecologist scheduled a follow-up appointment at eight weeks postpartum, but there was no real attention to my mental health. For those of you who gave birth during the pandemic, there's a good chance that the appointment took place over the phone. Actually, I *know* that appointment took place over the phone – because, in June 2020, I welcomed my third child – a baby girl. Even with my dark history, that appointment took place over the phone.

While there have been many instances in my life where I have felt lost– nothing brought my lost identity to light like being ill-prepared for motherhood.

And so, with a baby on my hip, I started my journey towards finding myself – a journey you might relate to. Maybe not all of it, perhaps only some – maybe none at all. Even if you can't relate to my depression or my health woes, or the chaos that ensued in my life, I know for sure you know a mother who can. Let this be your guide to support her.

12

WE DON'T EAT ORGANIC

I never wanted to be the mom that microwaved dinner or served Mac and Cheese daily for lunch. I thought I'd make everything from scratch, including baby food. And it would be organic. Obviously. Instead, my kids get chicken nuggets and fries three times a week. I'm not even sure if the chicken is antibiotic-free. It's frozen, from Wal-Mart, and off-brand, so I'm going to say that's a "no." I didn't want to be that mom, friends. Not that there's anything wrong with her – it's just not the mom I thought I would be. I also didn't want to be the mom that could never find a matching pair of socks. Or the mom whose floors couldn't be seen under a mess of toys and clothes and crumbs. Or the mom who would put on YouTube for two minutes (hours) of peace and freaking quiet. No ma'am. I did NOT want to be that mom.

I thought I would be the mom that would roll her own meatballs, make her own pasta sauce, and cut her own veggies (rather than buying them pre-sliced and in a tray). I wanted to have clean underwear in drawers, not in some random laundry basket by the stairs. I wanted to feel AT home with my babies, not just IN a home with my babies.

I wanted to make them feel loved with home-cooked food, tidy bedrooms, and desserts (that mommy made as a surprise…from scratch). I wanted to say "yes" to friends coming over after school without warning. I wanted to be the do-it-all-for-them mom. But what I've learned in only five short (long?) years of parenting is that the do-it-all-for-them mom is a farce. She doesn't exist. Unless you're my friend Nat, that girl is literally Martha Stewart meets Rachel Ray meets June Cleaver. She's the shit. And I might send my kids to live with her.

Me though? I'm not that mom. It doesn't matter how badly I want to be or how hard I try (and I try really damn hard). I get discouraged every time the clock strikes two and realize everything I set out to do hasn't been done. Maybe it's because I'm still in the trenches of motherhood (but truthfully…do we ever really climb out of them?). Maybe it's because every time one of my kids grows into a self-sufficient new phase, I have a toddler blooming right up behind them. Maybe it's because the moms of today just have too much crap on their plates.

I did (and do) want this life. With all of the good and bad moments that come along with these three little people, I love so darn much. So, while I may not be the mom I imagined I would be (I guess there's still time…), I have everything I ever dreamed of and a little bit more. I just hope I end up being enough for them. I hope the love and laughs and memories we make fill their bellies with the same kind of warmth that comes from their fresh bowl of Mac and Cheese. I really hope one day they look back on these times, thinking, "man, we had one hell of a childhood."

Because sometimes, I have to remind myself that this is *their* childhood. It's their one shot at magic and make-believe, and whimsical play. These are the years that will mold them and shape them. These years will be their years of nostalgia. These are the years that they get to do nothing more than be a kid. When they're running into my bed in the middle of the night – I often forget it's because they're looking to me for safety. When I'm breaking a sweat as I wrestle them into hats and mittens, I forget it's because they're excited about the snow. When they're screaming and crying and angry, I forget that it's because they have raw and unfiltered feelings.

Sometimes I get so caught up in being a parent and attempting to make every aspect of their childhood perfect that I forget what it means to be a kid. Some new moms think the Pinterest-perfect playroom, an adorable Pottery Barn nursery, and tiny miniature Nike's (that their 6-month-old will immediately kick off their feet) are things their baby actually needs. I'm serious. These aren't just items new moms pick out of thin air, people. New moms really believe that if they don't create a minimalist, Montessori playroom with a rotating toy shelf and ABC rug – their kid will be doomed. And don't even get me started on the Pottery Barn backpack, let alone the Pottery Barn nursery furniture. Seriously. I wish this backpack thing was a joke. But any time a mom asks what the best backpack is for their kid in a Facebook mommy group, the answer is always the $100 Pottery Barn backpack. Every freaking time. It's no wonder we're under so much stress to provide for our kids (and take on a side hustle…someone needs to pay for those backpacks).

Sometimes I forget that late-night snuggles and zipping zippers are all a part of their wonder and growth. I forget that the packing of picnics and hauling of sleds and long road trips (*are we there yet? I have to pee*) become some of their favourite core memories. Our walks around the block

– which aren't exactly a walk in the park…(if you know what I mean)…are really fun for them.

Being a mom is an integral part of my story – but childhood is **the most** important part of theirs. It's why I often regret not getting help for my postpartum depression sooner. Did my kids feel enough love when they were babies? Could they sense my panic? Did they know they were everything to me? I will never forgive myself for not getting help sooner. But I didn't know any better. No one talked about postpartum depression. And what I had heard made me terribly afraid that someone would take them away if I said anything and I would lose my babies. Even without asking for help, I still lost my babies at the hands of my thoughts and the turmoil in my mind. I missed out on enjoying so much of their babyhood. Depression stole so much from me, I just hope it didn't steal me from them.

As soon as we conceive our babies, we become a mother. And from that point forward, we're mothers for the rest of our lives. But our children have such a short time living their life as a kid – and yet, their childhood is what they'll remember the most.

So, I'm trying to let go of the type of mom I think I should be, and instead, trying to be the mom they need me to be. Which can be really hard to figure out – but I've been paying close attention to the things my kids ask of me, and they've shown me that what they need is really quite simple.

My kids have big feelings and need to feel validated. They like to lick the spoon when we make muffins, and they want to crawl into my bed at night because it makes them feel safe. My oldest son loves talking to me about video games, while my middle son squeals with excitement when I listen to him recite everything he knows about *Ghostbusters*. My daughter is happiest when she's on my lap or in my arms. Whenever Dave and I talk about moving into a larger home with more "functional" space, the kids loudly protest. Our home is home. Whether I feed them takeout or make them a homemade meal, they thank me for dinner. And at the end of the day, what they all really want is to be sleeping with their limbs wedged into my back. All the time I've spent trying to give them more than that hasn't done anything but stretch me far too thin in many aspects of my life and leaves me with an overwhelming sense of shame. As I've reached for more in these early years of motherhood, I forgot about the things that made me feel good – and most importantly, I forgot to live in the moment. That's a piece of time I'm never going to get back.

We can never go back in time, but we can make the most of the time we have left. By saying this, I don't mean you need to wake up with a pep in your step each and every day. You don't need to break open the windows and sing to the birds like Mary freaking Poppins. You don't even need to stop microwaving crap for your kids. I'm all about doing things that make life easier, and one of those things is letting go.

Here's what I mean by that. My house is a disaster. Every single room has stuff scattered about. It used to be a major trigger for my anxiety – and on days when I'm feeling overstimulated because I've taken on too much, it still is. Our beds are never made, and our laundry is never put away. I find tiny pants, pieces of Lego, socks, and random forks in places they don't belong. I tell my kids that people don't live like this. Friends can't spontaneously stop by. Every morning someone is missing something. I leave the house each day in a big huff. But one day, while sitting on the couch with a light dusting of crumbs under my butt – looking at the filth before me – I thought, "If it weren't messy, it would be clean…and that would be kind of sad." The truth is, I can't stand a messy house. It makes me crawl out of my skin. I've tried purging and organizing and using shelves and bins, and baskets. I'm really not sure if anyone else lives the way my family does. But one day, my house will be clean – a clean house will mean a quiet house. And as much as I love a quiet moment, I'm not ready for quiet to be my life. So, for now – I walk around the house (completely pointlessly), putting away socks and pants and forks and CRAP back in its place in exchange for hugs and goodnight kisses and tending to sweet little voices at their every beck and call. Because in my house, at least, you can't have one without the other. Motherhood has taught me that it's all about perspective.

13

HEY! YOU IN THERE!

Everything about pregnancy began and ended with me.
Except for conception. My husband likes to take the credit
for that – something about 'super sperm.' But at the end
of the day, I had the egg, the uterus, and the vagina. The
baby was in me. I don't want to discount the fact that men
may have their own set of struggles during pregnancy. I
know my husband was on the receiving end of some pretty
irrational requests and mood swings. But when we're
watching Carnival Eats and Treats, and I see a blooming
onion and say, "wow, that looks good," – that's his cue to
GO FIND ME ONE. If he couldn't catch on to my subtle
requests, that was his fault.

While pregnancy is usually a two-person experience,
the mom is the one at the heart of it. It's the mom with her
head in the toilet for nine months straight. The mom is the
one stripped down to nothing but a gown on a cold exam
table. The mom feels the little flutters of new life inside of
her. She makes the final call, hopefully with the support of
her partner, for invasive tests and emergency room visits.
And she has a (not always tiny) human exit her body at the
end of it all. Pregnancy is a beautiful thing that we get to

experience as the mom – when it all goes according to plan. But many times, for some reason or another, it doesn't.

After you get married (sometimes even before), people are invested in knowing when you're going to have a baby. I think I got asked at least five times at my very own wedding. I'm not sure if this is just something that happens with passionate Italians or if the rest of the world is still working on their manners – but these types of questions are not okay. The same thing happens after you have one child – everyone wants to know when you're giving them a sibling. Again folks, this type of questioning is not okay. You never know what's going on behind closed doors and what trigger you will hit. But if you're lucky enough to approach someone as blunt as me – you'll get the truth. Nothing but the awkward and uncomfortable cold, hard truth.

After experiencing the anti-unicorn pregnancy, I wasn't sure I could do the whole thing again. I knew for sure that I couldn't go another five months without knowing if I would lose my baby. I wasn't ready to hand over control and head into the unknown. I hadn't even come to grips with the idea that my first pregnancy resulted in a baby that was healthy and alive. I still had so much I needed to learn with Jack. And about me as a mom. I wasn't ready. After the chaos of my first pregnancy, I thought I was one and done. There was no way I thought I could handle the pregnancy thing again or the new mom thing again or navigate breastfeeding again. I couldn't do any of it again. My traumas, hemorrhoids, and extra baby weight were all still there. Still unaddressed. Still causing me pain. Another pregnancy brought too much uncertainty and too little sleep. Nope, I thought. We were one and done.

Then, Dave's twenty-ninth birthday rolled around, and

something about that day made me feel like I could do it all over again. Call it divine intervention, call it too much wine, or call it great sex, but there was nothing I wanted more than to make a baby. With bellies full of birthday cake and charcuterie, Dave and I 'left it up to God.'

Two weeks later, God handed me all-day nausea. With an eight-month-old baby on my hip and a positive pregnancy test in my hand, it was official; something greater decided it was time. That, or our Maxy was just one determined little swimmer.

Your mind races when you find out you're expecting. My mind always goes straight to labour. *That baby has to come out of me at the end of all this.* Then, once I come to accept that some part of me – whether it be my stomach or my vagina – is going to be ripped open, I move on to darker, more intrusive thoughts. Like the panic that comes with bringing a living, breathing human into the world. *It's cool, I can handle it.* Except I couldn't handle it. I wasn't equipped to handle it. I went from leaving it up to God, to believing in my heart of hearts that there was no way I could give two babies a full and happy life. I was lost.

In those first eight months of being a mom to Jack, I felt completely disconnected from myself, my family, and my friends. I felt disconnected from my career, my home, and my marriage, too. Everything, in some way, felt foreign. I didn't know who I was – all I knew was I had a responsibility as a mother now, so I didn't have a hall pass to figure it out. I couldn't throw in a time-out card and take a moment to find myself. That definitely couldn't happen if I became a mother of two. And while I never quite felt like I had found my place in life, I have never felt more lost than I did in those early years of motherhood.

You felt lost when you became a mom, too, right? If you did, then raise your hand. Now, place your hand over your heart. Close your eyes. Scratch that, finish reading this paragraph, and – then close your eyes. I want you to connect to that feeling of being lost. Identify where that feeling of loss is coming from. Because I need you to understand you didn't lose your identity to one singular thing. You didn't lose your identity just because you had a baby. There are so many reasons we lose bits and pieces of our identity throughout the course of our life. Especially in our younger years when we're not confident enough to tell people to fuck off.

Sitting in this very moment, you may still be overwhelmed with the feeling of being lost. There are so many factors that contribute to that feeling. Write them down. Identify the core reason behind it. Are you lost in your career? Maybe you're not pursuing your passion. Are you lost in your physical body? Maybe it's time to practice some more self-love. Are you lost in exhaustion and defeat? Maybe you need to figure out what balance *could* look like – and then ask for help. Motherhood amplifies our anxieties. It highlights all of our imperfections as we strive to create the perfect life for our babies. But our babies don't need us to be perfect – they just need us to be us.

Maybe you've already started peeling back your layers. Maybe you're just beginning to identify who you truly are. Maybe, it's only now that you've realized you're lost. There is a path forward, and we're both walking it together.

I made a promise to myself before I became a mom. I promised to give my all to my babies while not losing all of who I was to my babies. And over my years as a mother, I'd be lying if I didn't say bits and pieces of myself have been lost along the way. My flat tummy, full and thick hair and well-rested glow are just some of the many things that have changed. My marriage is almost unrecognizable. That could be a book in itself. Time is scarce and precious, and there's never enough of it. I have an entirely new group of friends. We call ourselves the 'Paw Patrollers.' Each of us has an assigned character – because why wouldn't women in their mid-thirties want to identify as a rescue pup? But those pups have saved the day a time or two. They cleaned me up when I puked in an Uber after attending my first concert post-pandemic. And they've helped me wrangle a kid or two into my house during really big meltdowns.

The way I used to be is gone. Bon voyage. See you never. I'm a more exhausted, often anxious, scruffier version of myself. So much of what I've lost in motherhood has been physical. The familiar way my clothes feel draped over my body, the familiar way my husband's hands feel wrapped around my skin. The visual and functional aspects of my physical self. However, when it comes to the other parts of me – my mind and spirit – all I can say is that my mental health wasn't lost in motherhood – it was uncovered.

For years, I had been fighting a mental health battle and was unwilling to get help. I had reasons and excuses for not bettering myself. For not pulling myself out of a hole. I blamed everything on my circumstances – instead of identifying my inability to cope with them. I didn't realize just how sick I was. With a near pre-term birth and the diagnosis of a rare tumor in one of my glands, pregnancy number two made it all come to a head. It put my life into perspective, and I had to evaluate what I was really running from in my life. Running from a fear of failure only chased me further away from myself. All I ever really wanted was to feel connected to me, so why was I trying so hard to be someone else?

Motherhood transformed me. It made me realize I had totally and completely lost myself to the expectations of others – which then became expectations I placed on myself. It also made me want to be the best version of myself. Not every woman needs to become a mother to come into their own or find themselves. But I needed to become a mom. I needed babies. As I helped my babies discover who they are in their world, it opened my eyes to mine.

If I had never had babies clinging to me every second of every day, I'm not sure I ever would have had a reason to find myself. I'll never really know.

Uncovering my true self took a lot of learning and unlearning. I had to peel back the layers of my onion. I had to heal. I had to understand each and every thing that brought me to a place of feeling such inadequacy. It was only then that I filled each hole from my past with something that truly represented me in the present moment.

14

GROUNDHOG DAY

Being home with kids all day can make you feel a little numb sometimes. Days often play out like Groundhog Day. Feed the baby, and have coffee. Feed the toddler, and have coffee. Wipe a butt, and have coffee. Turn on Paw Patrol, and have coffee. Deal with a tantrum…can you mix edibles and coffee? Naptime followed by coffee. The kids are awake; where is the coffee? Ask your husband when he's coming home from work, and have some more coffee. Sometimes days go more like this: tantrum, coffee, tantrum, coffee, tantrum, coffee. My kids liked to switch it up every once in a while, so I wouldn't get bored.

Being a stay-at-home mom taught me some tremendous real-world skills, however. Thanks to my kids, I can sense a meltdown like a service dog and talk down a said tantrum as police would in a hostage negotiation. If needed, I can wipe a butt as the rest of its body runs wild through a house. I can hold a baby in one arm, a toddler in another, and chop onions simultaneously without crying (it's probably because there are no tears left come dinner time but let me have this one). Other impressive skills: I've memorized all the words to "Goodnight Moon" and can be enthusiastic about absolutely anything.

Stay-at-home mom-life, it's not for the faint of heart. When my kids were toddlers, they spent most days in a diaper and one sock. That's it. No pants, no shirt, not even the other sock. I did the best I could under the circumstances. Getting a toddler dressed for the day is like trying to put pants on a thrashing alligator. Realistically, I probably could have gotten two socks on them. The pants, on the other hand, were much too ambitious. And that was just my kids, then there was my house. Actually, my house hasn't changed much since those early years of parenting. It's sticky and covered in a light dusting of crumb – and if you're going to come over, there are a few things you should know:

1. I can't guarantee you won't step on a toy.

2. Also, I can't guarantee you won't step on something sticky.

3. Basically, watch your step. The floor is lava. Use the pillows provided to safely transition from room to room.

4. Someone will fart in your personal space.

5. I'm not sure what that smell is. Yes, we've looked under the couch.

6. I don't have anything to feed you besides hotdogs and Goldfish crackers.

7. Are your ears sensitive to screeching? Because we have a lot of that here.

8. Welcome to the Jungle might start playing when you

walk in. I'm not sure why, it just happens.

9. We have a dog. He's been emotionally neglected and will hump you for attention.

10. Don't be scared and please come back. I need you.

It's chaos, friends. Raising kids is absolute mayhem. Especially in those early years of parenting because, plain and simple, toddlers simply don't give a fuck.

Most days, I couldn't wait for my husband to get home from work. It's not because my kids were "bad" or because I wanted to run free the second he strolled through the door – though, I must admit there was a time or fifty the thought crossed my mind. It wasn't even because I didn't love and cherish the time I had at home with my babies – although having someone else flush the toilet for you before you hop off was never really a trip to the spa. I couldn't wait for my husband to get home from work because here's the truth – I love being a mom when my husband is home. Like L-O-V-E love. There are three kids, two adults, and even though outnumbered, we do that whole live-laugh-love thing a little more fluidly than when I'm home alone. But when I'm home alone, I'm always stretched too thin, try to do something fun to occupy my kids and get myself in a messy situation.

Like, does anyone else try to do the "fun mom" thing? You know what I'm talking about – the paint, sensory bins, water, kinetic sand, and Play-Doh (all things I've come to ban from my home). That sort of stuff. It always seems like a good idea. You think to yourself, "Today is the day. Today I'm going to be that mom. I'm going to craft the shit out of this day." And then you confidently strut to the craft closet or the bucket or the nook, and you pull out all the fabulous goodies you picked up at the store after being inspired by something you saw on Pinterest. You actually believe your kids will sit and make a cute little caterpillar out of nothing more than an egg carton and pipe cleaners. Easy peasy. Or, oh my gosh – why not paint a giant mural? Your little Picasso can put his tiny, sticky, paint-craving hands to good use.

Yes. Craft days are so fun. You were made to be a craft mom. So, you roll out a big (and I mean BIG) sheet of paper for your kids to paint all over. They won't be able to miss it. The floor will be saved. And you get them some water to clean off their brushes. It's perfect, the most fun day. Except your kid dumps all the water on their head, paints all over the floor, and leaves you with a giant friggin mess.

You wonder where the heck it all went wrong. Was it the water? The paint? Should you have done all of this *after* their nap? You vow never to be a #craftmom again. And then lo and behold, one rainy Tuesday when your husband is at work, and you're home alone with your kids….

Truthfully, I live for the weekends when we can do the family thing. Where I'm not the maid, nanny, mom, chauffeur, chef, and everything in between. Kidding. I'll be that for the rest of my life. But it helps to have my husband home with me. We tag-team the chaos together. I shower and feel a bit more like myself.

Monday always rolls around again, though – and I turn back into a disorganized, unshowered pumpkin to face another week.

15

YOUR IDENTITY ISN'T WITHIN AN MLM (UNLESS IT IS, THEN GET IT, QUEEN)

One of the most anxiety-inducing parts of motherhood – besides the first postpartum poop – is returning to work after maternity leave. Thinking about my first day back in the office literally made me sick. And I thought about it a lot. Basically, every day. From the moment I found out I was pregnant to the moment I was on the delivery table... and every moment afterward. In true Annie fashion, I developed a hyper-fixation on returning to work. I hyper-fixated on every scenario that could get me out of it. I'm not kidding – at one time, I even considered selling my own underwear on Craigslist. This was before *Only Fans*. People had to get creative.

While I didn't mind my job, I wasn't a huge fan of my career. I wasn't 'living the dream' by any means. I had an average job at an average company in an average cubicle. My commute, however, was stellar. An entire five-minute drive from home… and ten minutes to the nearest HomeSense. It allowed for some pretty spectacular work-life balance. However, this type of work-life balance wasn't going to cut it for me anymore. A short commute to home, while a perk, simply wasn't enough. Having a baby changed everything.

I was most nervous about handing my baby over to a stranger. Daycares are vetted and stuff – but could I *really* trust them? Then, there was the reality that I was sending my kid to daycare only to go off and make money for 'The Man.' Daycare was (is) expensive. When all was said and done, I'd bring home about half of my salary – and for what? So we could eat the *fancy* canned beans? No thanks. Another factor in my anxiety was that I didn't really care about my line of work…or the whole working nine-to-five thing in general. I wanted something flexible. I felt called to do something else. Something bigger than I was...but I didn't quite know what that meant.

Thus began the hyper-fixation on finding a work-from-home job. Which lead to a hyper-fixation with #bossbabes and their Instagram profiles. Which led to hyper-fixation with residual income. Which made me believe the only way I could: stay home, raise babies, keep my house clean, make money, and have any kind of value as a stay-at-home mom was to join a multi-level marketing company. I became obsessed with chasing that picture-perfect life. I had to be like them if I wanted to be happy. I had to be like the moms who had it all, did it all, and got to do it all from their own home in a cute top knot.

As the months closed in on my mat leave, my anxiety reached a level I had never experienced before. I was angry and resentful. I was mad that my husband and I didn't save more money before we had children. I was resentful of myself for chasing that stupid old boyfriend and messing up my education. I hyper-fixated over every decision I had ever made in my life, looking to place blame. And you can bet your bottom dollar that I found plenty. All of it was my fault, of course. I needed a way to supplement my income if I was going to stay home. I began to Google ways to make money as a stay-at-home mom. I also turned to the ever-so-popular 'Mommy Facebook Groups' to hear from 'real' success stories. I could take pizza orders from home. I could transcribe documents from home. I could even clip coupons from home. But the one consensus that guaranteed I was going to make it 'big' was that I had to become one of 'them.' One of those moms who lived in a constant state of hustle. The hustling mom. Such a twenty-first-century concept. I mean, I remember my mom dragging me to a good ole Tupperware party back in the day. The tuna salad and crackers at those things were divine. But the lifestyle of those mothers didn't reflect anything like what we see today. They weren't climbing the MLM ladder to get free vacations or a white Mercedes Benz. They weren't snail-mailing the neighbourhood moms photos of their extravagant trips. They didn't promise a sisterhood. They just fucking liked Tupperware, and they were trying to make a few bucks. There weren't any big promises.

Our generation is full of promises. Big ones. For millennial moms – especially those who loathe their careers and therefore feel incapable of leaving their babies – the MLM life is the OUT. Oils, makeup, some sort of miracle wrap. I had to become a multi-level marketing machine mom. Or sell something on Etsy. But I'm about as crafty as a twig.

Being someone who lives with anxiety, I had to overanalyze the pros and cons of the whole ordeal. The best and worst-case scenario of everything. What would happen if I didn't go back to my job? What would the cost of two kids in daycare look like? What would, could, and *should* happen? MLM life promised me a sisterhood unlike any other. My upline (the person who recruited me into the MLM) promised me that I would be welcomed into a team of women who would uplift and support me – not just in my business but in motherhood as well. It was the career that promised a sense of belonging and friendship, something I had searched for my entire life.

The cons: I hated the concept of multi-level marketing. As soon as I became a mom, it seemed like anyone and everyone in the industry was knocking on my door. Any time someone from high school reached out to tell me about a business opportunity, I cringed. This isn't to say I don't want to support my friends or acquaintances in their endeavors; I do. And I have many friends who passionately work in direct marketing and are kicking butt at it – because it's *their* thing. If essential oils are your passion, hand to God, I encourage you to chase your dream (just do your research first). It wasn't my thing, though, and people who could benefit from it tried to convince me otherwise. I didn't want to force myself out of my comfort zone. Sales weren't my thing, but the future filled with promise was. A future filled with promise meant I got to stay at home with my babies.

With hesitation, I signed on with a popular essential oil company. I was the perfect candidate for this type of job. I was feeling totally and completely lost, and more so, I was looking for someone to validate me. As a mom, I didn't have an "out." I couldn't go back to school or change my career overnight. I couldn't call a time-out and take a moment to figure out who I was, let alone what I wanted to do with my career. But what I could do was hustle my butt off during naptime, evenings, and weekends and make this MLM thing work. I bought into their message, their brand, and their promise of a better life for myself and my family. I bought into the sisterhood. And I mean, I literally bought in. I purchased products and stock; I bought the membership, and I bought little samples and cute stationery to mail to my friends. I convinced myself that I had to make it work or go back to my typical nine-to-five.

For four months I hustled my little stretch-marked bum off. Learning everything there was to know about essential oils. Lavender is great for headaches, peppermint works well for tummy aches, and frankincense is the miracle oil that will leave your skin flawless. I had my own pitch, my own presentation, and my very own small audience. Yet, I made no money. I did, however, 'invest' some of my family's money in this little company of mine. But an investment only works if there's a return, right?

I watched others on my team appear to succeed as they flashed their fancy essential oil hustle all over social media. The MLM lifestyle. A photo of a diffuser in a clean kitchen. A picture of a mom and her baby playing in an adorable playroom. An image of a redacted cheque and some fluffy statement about that mama feeling, "oh so #grateful." It was everywhere. Somehow, they were making it work. It could have been a fake-it-till-they-made-it approach, or they could have been thriving. If they were thriving, it's probably because they were pursuing something that genuinely filled their cup. But for me, this was just another thing I was failing at. The mom-boss life wasn't the life for me – and I was running out of time.

As I put more money into my business – not getting one cent back – it was clear that I was going to face the day I had dreaded since my baby was born. A day when I would bring Jack, my one true love besides my husband, to a facility. I'd leave him in the arms of a stranger while I spent my day in a cubical making money for The Man. I was bitter. I was resentful. Truthfully, I was a mess.

Returning to work after maternity leave was exactly as

hard as I thought it was going to be. It could have been because I went back to work twenty weeks pregnant. My emotions and hormones were all over the map. One minute I was happily sipping hot chocolate at my desk, while the next, I was sobbing to a slideshow of my baby's photos paired with a Sarah McLachlan soundtrack. Each day was an emotional rollercoaster. Friends and family told me it would get easier. They said dropping Jack off at daycare would get easier. That we would all eventually find our groove in our new schedule. That I would eventually find balance, and my energy would be restored. It wouldn't be this hard forever. While each situation is different – it never got easier for me. In fact, my time back at work was one of the more challenging periods in my life. This comes from a woman writing two years into a pandemic. The return after mat-leave is hard stuff, and for me, there were a few reasons why.

First and foremost, daycares are a Petri dish. They're a colourful and disgusting little breeding ground for everything from hand, foot, and mouth disease to the common cold. Within Jack's first month in daycare, he was sick so often that I had to use every last hour of my vacation time to nurse him back to health. His little body battled everything from ear infections, colds, flu, and even the infamous hand, foot, and mouth disease. A smorgasbord of viruses hit our home within the span of a month. All of which my husband and I ended up catching, too. Friends told us daycare helps to build up your immune system. Cool. But that doesn't make it any easier when shit is *literally* hitting the fan.

The second reason going back to work was hard was because I was twenty weeks pregnant. Growing a set of arms and legs and the entire anatomy for another human being is hard work. It's exhausting. That month-and-a-half back at the office really did me in. Every day after work I made a homecooked meal, I kept up with cleaning the house, I tried to find time to connect with my husband. Then there was my son, who needed attention. And my friends who wanted to go out for coffee. It was all too much, and I couldn't keep up. My expectations were too high. Good ole June Clever couldn't even meet them. The balance just wasn't there.

And the last reason I had a hard time going back to work – my heart was in another place. It wasn't at this job I was holding onto to help pay our bills, it was with my son, who had yet to stop crying when I dropped him off at daycare. It was with my dishes piled in the sink, causing me immense anxiety. It was with the expectations I set for myself to be a kick-ass mom. It was with my sweatpants and my couch and my bed. It was with those dreams that the soft voices were calling me to follow.

Every moment I was away from my son caused me physical pain, and it caused me to make a rash and harsh decision. A decision that makes sense today. A decision that completely changed the course of my career. Six weeks into doing the working mom thing, I walked out on my job. It brought a little piece of my authenticity forward. It was a step in the right direction. However, at the time, all I felt was guilt and shame. Walking away from my career was a huge sacrifice. The sole financial burden would fall on my husband – our bills, our mortgage, our two kids, everything. I also felt guilt over how I left my job – I honestly could never go back…and I'd be lucky if I could use them as a reference. Then I tried to understand why the working-mom thing never got easier for me. I tried to understand why I wasn't able to sacrifice time with my son to make my career work. Other women seemed to be able to leave their babies at daycare and return to their careers.

Other women seemed to adjust. Some women seemed to even like the time away from home. Why wasn't it working out for me?

Five years later, on the flip side of the hardest six weeks of my life, it all makes sense. I couldn't return to work because I wasn't being true to myself. I thought I wasn't capable enough to have a career and be a mom when really, it was that my career wasn't *enough* for me. I had gone so long trying to fit into a role that was never meant to be mine. Each job I've ever taken was a pivot. A step towards where I was meant to be. That wouldn't become clear until everything finally aligned. Until I eventually sacrificed the right things. I would never have left my career if there wasn't something more important pulling for my attention. It just happened to be my son. My son is part of my story and my journey, and he's the reason I started to find my way. He made me realize I was so resistant to leaving him because I was sacrificing the wrong things at that time.

Sacrifice is a concept that comes up repeatedly for moms. It's like as soon as we become a mom, we're being called to sacrifice something. And the truth is, we are. Mothers sacrifice in an endless number of ways. My career was an epiphany in the way I look at sacrifice. As a result, I've stopped seeing sacrifice as something bad, and I've started seeing sacrifice as the direct result of time not being right. I've learned that sacrifice is really the universe making space for us to realign and learn. When I returned to work, I was broken because I thought I had to sacrifice time with my son. Really, it was time to do just the opposite. At that moment in my life, I was supposed to sacrifice my career. It's why I felt completely out of alignment. It's why I was such a wreck.

Sacrifice isn't and should never be at the cost of losing

who you truly are. Sacrifice shouldn't make you feel physically ill. It should be an awakening. Sacrifice is an opportunity to reevaluate the purpose and direction of your life. It's for your greater good, not the greater good of others. I've learned that the universe only makes you sacrifice when you've loaded too much on your plate. When you're being called to sit and tune in to a particular moment. SO, whatever you've been called to sacrifice – whether it's sacrificing your career, your friendships, your time, or your body, it's only because the universe is making room for something bigger and better. Just tune into the power of your instinct and move when you're called. Only you will know when it's time. Remember that soft voice? If you listen, you'll hear it whisper exactly what you need to hear.

I knew it was time to sacrifice. It's why I walked out on my career without notice. I closed a door behind me that could never be reopened but at the same time, I was opening a door that aligned with my purpose. And while, yes, my husband and I had to make sacrifices to our spending habits – my purpose eventually came to light and everything – finances, time away from my babies, my sense of fulfillment – aligned back to center.

16

KNOCK KNOCK, IT'S YOUR SPIRIT CALLING

I can safely say, since becoming a mother, I've had an awakening. I've awakened every two hours, every night, for the last five years. It's been a treat. A real knee-slapper. But besides waking up with my kids, I've awakened in another way, too. The kind of awakening that rocks your soul like a hurricane. I've awakened my spirit.

When I walked away from my career – without anything but parenting to fall back on – I had time to reflect on my life. At all hours of the night. Covered in all kinds of drool and goober. And that reflection took me to a few different places in what I like to call my self-reflection tour.

The first stop on my tour was a place of regret. I reassessed my life from my earliest memories to my most present, and I picked apart every single moment I went wrong. From my Kappa tearaway tracksuit to graduating from university with a three-year pass rather than a four-year degree, I criticize myself over my decisions. Regret. Regret. Regret.

My biggest regret takes me back to age seventeen. I had

just started to come into my own and was casually seeing a guy from the football team. In an effort to be "cool" and get in with his friends, I invited them to spend a weekend at my family's tiny rustic cottage. A cottage my dad and my grandparents built with their own two hands. The furniture has my teething marks on it, and the carpet is a thick seventies shag. To me, it's home. To a group of wild teenagers, it's a party destination.

One sunny Saturday, cars loaded with teenagers and beer arrived at our little neck of the woods. My parents looked on from the deck, insisting they tag along to oversee the fun. It was going to be wholesome. I was going to show my new crew of friends the trails and the best fishing spots and maybe even sneak in a drinking game or two when my folks went off to bed. Except I had never really partied with this group of friends before. From sun up to sun up – that's not a typo, they never went to sleep – this group of frat-like teens was drinking their way through cases of beer.

In an effort to scatter in some old-timey cottage fun, I took a few of the guys fishing. There were fewer casualties when I brought toddlers fishing for the first time. One of the guys broke the boat. One of the guys broke my dad's fishing rod. And none of them could bait their own hook. Back at the cottage, another one of the guys overflowed our toilet with his number two and left it for my mom to clean up in a drunken stupor. Since we had guests, she had to use her good towels.

Then, there was the fact that nobody brought a single piece of food. We could stock an entire Beer Store with our inventory, but they didn't bring one single thing to eat. My parents nearly went into debt feeding that rabid group of football players. The entire weekend was a disaster. Hands down the most embarrassing moment of my life.

Even compared to that time I accidentally shit my pants in front of my husband in the car. There is nothing I regret more than what went down that weekend at a place that's so sacred and precious to me. It truly is my only life regret. Every other thing that's gone wrong in my life has led me to where I am today – the place I was always supposed to be.

The second stop on my reflection tour was a place called FOMO. I had an intense Fear Of Missing Out. What was I afraid of missing out on? Anything and everything. Many of my friends were still childless, and if they weren't childless, they were either expecting or parenting one little munchkin. Many of my "maternity leave friends" had returned to the office where they were making money and wearing nice clothes, and going on work lunches. While I was changing up to fifteen diapers a day, my friends were on girls' trips without guilt and sexy date nights that ended with…well, sex. They were glowing and refreshed. I had a leaky bladder and postpartum bald spots.

There were days when I felt trapped. I could never (and still never) find the time to do it all. To cook and clean and wrestle with my babies on the floor. If the only thing wrong in a day was my house smelling like poop, then I considered myself lucky. There was always a stink, whether it was a long-lost diaper or a sippy cup full of milk that someone hid like Blackbeard's treasure. There wasn't a single essential oil that could cover the smell. Then there was the laundry. The piles and piles and piles of laundry. It got to a point where I didn't even bother hanging it up in our closets anymore. I would pull a clean pair of undies right from the dryer and go on with my day. And my kids? I was that mom whose kids were always running around in their diapers. I remember a neighbour once asked me, "Why aren't your kids ever wearing any clothes?" Because clothes mean laundry, Karen. That's why. (Her name was actually Karen).

There was never enough time. Then there were our financial struggles. The ones that seemed to be pilling upon us like our bills. We signed up for a big ole mortgage at the top of our affordability when we had two incomes. It was the only way we could squeeze into the just-outside of Toronto suburbs. At the time, the home was close to both of our careers. It checked everything off our list. It worked for us as two newly married, childless adults. But after two kids, all it did was gouge our paycheques and drive me mad.

I fully acknowledge that these are First World problems. And since medication, meditation, and my awakening, I've changed my way of thinking. I've watched endless hours of videos on YouTube trying to train myself to be grateful, mindful, and appreciative – the works. But the stay-at-home mom gig? It became pretty isolating. My mind went down a deep hole that took a while to climb out of.

The third stop on my reflection tour was a place of panic. Oh my, there was panic. Here I was, a stay-at-home mom with my beautiful babies and a loving husband – and I found endless things to panic about. Now, before I go down the rabbit hole, I have to give myself some compassion – my pregnancies were complex and resulted in mental health issues. Neither of which was my fault. The way postpartum depression made me react to my surroundings is also not my fault. But it was all-consuming until I got help – and the thing that consumed me the most was our home.

Our cute and quaint 1,500-square-foot townhome in the suburbs was supposed to be our five-year plan. We would spend a year throwing swanky parties as DINKS (double income, no kids), then have two kids, two-ish years apart, and finally, make our move into a bigger home when our five years were up – just in time to welcome our third child. Except life went a little more like this: have two high-risk pregnancies in under a year and a half. BOOM. We fast-tracked the plan.

As you know, I'm a person who appreciates when things go according to plan. When the plans derail – I derail. It's a messy trainwreck and includes hyper-fixation, anxiety, and beads of sweat. So, v. This pregnancy would, of course, cause a ripple effect. We'd have to move up the conception of baby number three if we were to stay on track. But our house had no room for our growing family. As a stay-at-home mom, the home was my place of business, and I needed it to work with the plan. I needed it to help my day flow and move along easily – because raising babies is hard enough.

Our laundry room was in the basement. This meant lugging heavy bins of laundry down two flights of stairs while my babies… – wait? Where would I leave my babies? How could I do laundry in a dusty, unfinished basement with two kids under two? With the laundry in the basement, this meant we didn't have a mudroom on the main floor. WHERE WOULD THE SNOW PANTS GO? How could I host magical, memory-making birthday parties with no dining room to serve my appetizers in? And how could I make my mark as a writer with no office? And oh my gosh, we only had a single-car garage. WHERE WOULD THE BIKES AND WAGONS GO? But wait, I had just quit my job. How would we get approved for a mortgage? We'd have to move to a more affordable city. But it would be further from Dave's work. And Dave didn't want to move further from his work. Screw Dave. We had to move.

See? Obsession, anxiety, and panic (in the most first-world ways, but gosh, it was all-consuming for me).

Imagine living with that. Not only from my perspective, with all of those thoughts swirling through my head – they were all-consuming. But imagine what it was like to live through that as Dave…sorry baby.

I lost it, friends. The panic sank in. The chaos of the toys, and the things, and all the children I didn't even have yet, consumed me. Dave will tell you; that it consumed me.

While I was wallowing in pity and FOMO, and regret – my sweet little fetus was growing impatient. Nudging me here, kicking me there, causing tight and regular contractions almost daily. Around thirty weeks pregnant, things really ramped up. My contractions weren't just twitchy anymore – they were painful, and I couldn't get them to stop.

A quick visit to Labour and Delivery indicated Max was way, way down low in my cervix. He was breech, and the on-call OBGYN could feel his bum with the tips of her fingers. I was also two centimeters dilated and eighty percent effaced. While it's common to loosen up earlier in your subsequent pregnancies, my baby was getting ready to fall out. I was immediately transferred by ambulance to a high-risk hospital in Toronto, where I spent two weeks on bed rest.

Each day, Dave and I met with the neonatal intensive care unit, pediatric specialist, and high-risk obstetrics teams – and each day, they told us the stats of delivering our baby early. Underdeveloped lungs, learning disabilities, blindness. And just like that, I had a second traumatic pregnancy on my plate, distracting me from all of the petty concerns I had circling through my head back home.

Those days in that hospital room were the first time I ever had to split myself between my children. It was the first time I felt spread too thin. It was the first time I had to choose between two of my kids. And I can tell you, three kids later, stretching myself between them happens a lot.

While I ached and hurt and guiltily grappled with myself, I focused on surviving. But what I've since learned through the hard, harder, and hardest moments of my life is that moments like this aren't about survival – they're about perspective. The FOMO and regret, and panic, are all about perspective, too. If I was just able to change my perspective, then just maybe I would've connected with myself sooner. But no regrets, right?

Perspective isn't always enough on its own, and maybe sometimes you have to survive in the moment, but simple shifts in our thinking can bring enough optimism to make it to the next day. Or possibly even learn a lesson.

Hard things happen in life, and they often don't make any sense. Many times, we question why bad things happen to good people or why bad things happen to innocent people, or why bad things happen at all. While the reasons for the pain are often entirely unfair – we don't grow in this life unless we experience pain. This isn't to say we deserve pain or that people we love deserve pain. No one deserves pain – however, for some reason, pain is a part of our life. It's what we do with that pain that can honour the people we love or even ourselves.

In the midst of panicking about all of the things I couldn't change, life was about to hand me perspective on a platter – a whole lot of hard on a big stinking plate. And this is the part of my story where I collapse. Where all I can do is survive day-to-day, hour-to-hour, and minute-to-minute. But when I came out of that survival, I came out with perspective, a place where grief and gratitude could co-exist. I had my awakening.

17

DON'T CALL ME IN AN EMERGENCY

I'm afraid of flying. Terrified. So much so that I don't fly – not for my honeymoon, not to Disneyland, and not even to be Annie in Paris. Okay, that's a lie. When I was twenty-three, Dave took me on a 45-minute flight to New York City. To prepare, I drank a few too many beers in the airport bar. Once we boarded, I had to pee, and in a drunken stupor, I pleaded to go to the bathroom while a U.S. Marshal threatened to escort me off the plane. I haven't flown since.

With this in mind, I've never been on any *real* adventures. I haven't ziplined, bungee jumped, or ridden a hot air balloon through a sunny sky. I *have* stood in line for eight hours for Build-A-Bear's pay-your-age day. Talk about adventure!

Besides paying a dollar for a Build-A-Bear, I believe the greatest and most important adventure in our lives is discovering who we really are. You never know who's hanging out behind the cobwebs of self-doubt until you start sweeping them away. What I'm talking about here is not self-care. Depending on the stage of parenting you're in, self-care can be total bullshit. Let alone finding the time for self-care. And the guilt that comes with self-care. And the little fingers under the door that come with self-care. While self-care has its place at the end of a long day, a bubble bath here or there isn't going to awaken the fierce spirit inside of you. Healing from your traumas and getting in touch with who you really are – that's where the magic happens.

But what's the difference between self-care and self-discovery, Annie? Good question. I couldn't tell the difference for a while, either. Are you ready for the secret sauce? Grab a pen and write this down…the difference is *how it makes you feel.* *Mic drop* Self-care is an instant, time-limited gratification, while self-discovery is like climbing Everest. It's hard to breathe, your heart works a little harder, you get queasy and nauseous – but once you reach the top: ecstasy (and tingly hands and feet, from what I've heard).

Self-discovery isn't about finding moments of joy; it's about living a life you feel joyful in. It's an ongoing process that strips away anything unimportant. It requires you to examine your own thoughts, words, and actions. It leads you to a life lived with intention. Self-discovery is important because it shows us how we've failed to identify with our true selves, and allows us to start rectifying that. Living out of alignment with ourselves can distort our experiences and lead to mental health struggles like depression.

When I was twenty-two, my dad had his hip replaced. It came about two years too late. The man hobbled around until he ticked every last task off his clipboard checklist. When I wonder why I'm so Type-A, I don't have to think for long. I'm just like my dad. I know it, he knows it – my mom knows it. I'm just like him. And because of that, I think he understands me better than I know myself. After years of learning and growing and overcoming, my dad has let the tough-guy persona go and became a zero-fucks-left kind of guy. I hope that one day, I give as few fucks as he does. He makes it all seem pretty great.

After checking every last item off his list, my dad eventually had his surgery. After only forty-five minutes under the knife, he had a new ceramic hip and was, "good for the next thousand miles," as he would say.

Hospital post-op care was supposed to last a week. Stable vitals and physiotherapy goals had to be met. But my dad's a madman – he's gritty, and he's fierce. And if you tell him he can't do something, he only does it faster. So, when the doctor said he had to climb the stairs before going home, my dad climbed the stairs on day one. By day two, he was walking the halls. *Does this sound like hyper-fixating to you?* He was pushing the limits all due to a greater plan: to break out of the hospital early and watch the Grey Cup.

There are a few things you should know about my dad. One, my dad worked hard for the money, so he doesn't pay extra for anything. He also steals change from other people's counters, so if you're inviting him over – lock that shit up. For only twenty-five dollars, a nurse could have wheeled the Grey Cup to the base of his hospital bed, but that was twenty-five dollars too much. The second thing you should know is that my dad had incredibly low blood pressure after surgery. It was so low that he nearly fainted while hiking it up those stairs. But it didn't matter because of…football.

With a fierce determination and a flexible nurse, my dad came home two days after surgery, just in time for the Grey

Cup. And during the Grey Cup, he went unconscious and nearly died in my arms. Not my dad, not the nurses, and not even the doctors knew that his low blood pressure was the result of an adverse reaction to pain medication. I was the one that filled his prescription. Thankfully, an angel dressed as a pharmacist gave us a general warning, "These things are strong. Have your dad start with one and take it from there."

Once we got my dad home from the hospital and into his bedroom – with a free TV at the base of his bed – my mom helped him change into something flowy and comfortable. A post-anesthesia sweat was trickling out of his pores while the incision on his thigh began to burn. It was impossible to get him into sweatpants, so my mom dressed him in one of her lacy satin nightgowns – it was the closest thing to a bathrobe she could find lying around. To this day, she claims it's because it was breathable. I say it's simply because she could.

There was my dad. Tucked in all cozy in his queen-size bed, wearing one of mom's nightgowns while watching the Grey Cup. He was living his best life, despite the whole new hip thing. I walked up to him, kissed him on the cheek, and handed him one Percocet. Then went off to grab something to eat.

For every major football event, we order pizza and wings. That day was no different. As I bit into a piece of gooey, cheesy goodness, my mom ran out of my parents' bedroom, past me, and to the phone. I don't remember what she said, but I ran to the back of the house to find my dad convulsing in a chair. His eyes were rolled back, and his jaw was stiff. I remember grabbing his face and feeling his cold skin.

My brother, Ricky, jumped into action and calmly pulled my dad onto the floor to begin CPR. My mom relayed information to the 911 dispatcher over the phone. I screamed confessions at my dad for every single thing I had ever done wrong. If he was leaving this earth, I needed him to know I was sorry for that time I broke a random glass in '95. Clearly, I am not the person you want by your side in an emergency.

Between Ricky, my mom, and the 911 dispatcher, my dad came back to us. And when he finally came back to us, he pulled himself up off the floor and dragged himself back to bed with one working hip and his nightie trailing behind. He was not going back to the hospital. The Grey Cup was on.

As soon as the paramedics arrived, I ran to a closet, shut the door, and lost complete control. While the paramedics, my mom, my dad, and my brother laughed at the lace nightgown, I cried like he never made it back to us. I unraveled from what could have been. And I carried that way of coping through to motherhood.

The birth of my babies, after having traumatic pregnancies, was exactly like my dad coming back from the dead. For everyone around me, it was a near miss. A miracle. Something I should have been eternally grateful for. But what they couldn't see parallel to my gratitude was trauma.

Not many people know that two Percocet would have killed my dad that day. Just like not many people know the types of conversations Dave and I had with our prenatal teams. Yes, the ending was happy – but getting there was super damn hard. Before my dad was alive, he was dead. Before Jack was viable, he was unlikely. Before Max was full-term, he was a pre-term baby on life support. At the moment, these were all very real things that were happening to me. And they didn't come with a warning, they happened on a bright sunny day when I thought everything was fine. I constantly held my breath, waiting for the other shoe to drop.

As everyone calmly rallied around our babies and as they calmly sat in our chaos, I watched in panic. Unraveling at the thought of what could have been. And when everyone had everything under control – whether it was my husband on a late-night feed or my parents dropping off a warm meal – I would hide in the back of my closet, lose complete control, and cry.

In the back of that closet, on my darkest day, I started my journey of self-discovery – though I didn't know it yet. I was dripping with babies and oozing with depression as the other shoe dropped closer to the ground. The U.S. Marshal was about to escort me off the plane. I was too fragile to be flying. But as it turns out, that's the best time to leap into the unknown.

18

PULLING THE BACKUP PARACHUTE

Kids are a magnet for conversation, and it all starts when you're pregnant. From your family to your co-workers to total strangers, everyone has something to say. And most of it sucks. None of it is ever helpful…even if it *is* helpful. (Don't hate me, but really, sleep when the baby sleeps).

As a new mom, I was aching to find another mom to chat with. I was also aching for solidarity. And to do that, I did what most mothers do, I preyed on families at the park. There were certain criteria I looked for when sourcing a potential mom-friend. Her kids had to be roughly the same age as mine. I typically looked for someone who was alone – sans other mom-friends, as it gave me an easier way in. And then I'd ask myself a series of important and distinctive questions like, are her shoes sneakers or flip-flops? Is her hair washed, or is that dry shampoo? And the big one: *Do you think she gets it?* There was only ever one way to find out. I'd wait for the mom to open her picnic lunch and then stealthily send my kids over to mooch.

After my kids had bellied up to the bar to get their hands on a Bear Paw, I'd dig into my bag of conversation starters.

The typical go-to's that every mom has – how old are your kids? How long have you lived in the area? What's your favourite pizza place? These are the basics and generally help you identify if you're in the same season of life. From there, the conversation would grow. We'd talk about things like sleep, work, our relationships…and I really thought it was only a matter of time until I could find someone who just *got* it.

But here's the thing – my kids, bless 'em, had some tough moments during those early years. And as for me? I was battling undiagnosed postpartum depression. While I could relate with moms about a lot of things – I was always the mom who had it harder, and it started to feel like my life reflected a slew of bad luck. I began to feel embarrassed about my story – and while I loved the happy-go-lucky conversation that came with meeting moms at the park, I was dying to talk to someone who understood me. And they just weren't there. That, or some people have a filter – unlike me – and aren't willing to bare all within minutes of meeting a stranger. *Oh, your pregnancy and baby and your life are #blessed? You don't scream into a pillow every night? Cool, cool, cool, me neither.* They didn't get it.

There's a powerful quote by bestselling author, podcaster, and mom of three Glennon Doyle Melton. She says this about an experience during a mommy playdate, "OK, so I don't know a lot about science, but I know that there are two different kinds of volcanoes. The first volcano is an active volcano and the second one is a dormant one. The dormant volcano looks calm on the outside, but inside, she's bubbling with boiling hot lava that, at any moment, could just explode and kill everyone in the vicinity. That's how I feel as a stay-at-home mom all day." The other mothers responded with stunned silence and wide eyes.

And Glennon thought, "Oh. We're not doing that here." We're not talking about the things we feel.

Glennon gets it. What Glennon said is exactly what I needed to hear. I needed to meet Glennon at that park in those early years, and I needed Glennon to sit in the yuck with me.

My greatest of luck, or whatever you want to call it, was that my boys were born miraculously healthy despite it all. And yet, the trend of isolation seemed to continue for me. I couldn't connect with other new moms who had babies who slept or had uncomplicated pregnancies. It was triggering for me.

So, unsurprisingly, the attitude of happy-go-lucky new mamas was hard for me to tolerate. I just couldn't relate to their positive experiences. Motherhood felt like jumping out of an airplane and having my parachute fail. I was standing on the edge of the plane's cabin, looking down at the ground below. Except I couldn't see the ground below because my eyes were clouded with tears. I'd paced back and forth, convincing myself it would all go according to plan. People jumped out of planes all the time – and even then, there was an instructor tied to my back.

My heart filled with butterflies as I prepared to throw myself into thin air…or, in this case, throw myself into parenting two kids under two after living through two traumatic pregnancies.

This is the part of motherhood where I began my freefall. I made the jump – everything else was out of my hands. For some of us, the leap is euphoric. You feel like a weightless piece of paper as you travel closer to the ground, eager to make the journey down. For others, jumping off the plane implies a point of no return, and that creates panic. This was me. As a new mom of two, I was panicked, even though I had support. I was told deploying the parachute would slow me down for a smooth descent. But why was I still traveling so fast? When I finally looked up, I saw my parachute flailing unopened in the wind.

Depression wasn't just a failed parachute in my postpartum story, it was an entire free fall toward death. I was terrified as I lost control of my feelings. The ground was getting closer, and I was hurtling toward it at full speed. Dave was my co-pilot...my instructor...and he grabbed onto me, trying to fix whatever had gone wrong.

When I finally had my second baby at thirty-eight weeks, I was overcome with grief after getting home from the hospital. From the outside looking in, you couldn't find a logical reason why. Two beautiful boys – healthy as could be. If anything – the only thing I should have been feeling was grateful. But that's when the floodgates opened.

Since becoming a mom, I've become the type of person who collapses when things get good. It's in the calm where I face my darkest demons. Because when things are chaotic, I don't have a choice but to hold on for my babies. When life is spinning, I want them to be able to look at me and know they're safe. The chaos is where I find myself most resilient. But when the dust settles - when life steadies, and our family has its feet firmly on the ground, I fall apart. It's become a trend for me. Strong as fuck during our hardest moments and frail when life is at its best. And I think it's because when things are hard - especially when you're a mom, you're not just holding on for yourself. You're holding on for your family. You're masking the moment with an assurance that everything will be okay. But when things are good? The only expectation is that you remain grateful.

Unfortunately for me, being grateful isn't enough to keep me from falling apart. Because here's the thing, you can be grateful and still be healing from trauma. You can be grateful and be terrified that the other shoe will drop. You can be grateful and still live with moments of depression. And it's often when we're in our most grateful moments, in those moments that flow to us with ease, that we find ourselves face to face with the darkness we suppressed. And we break. Yes, some of us only break when things are good - because it's the only time we can.

For two years, I had been a bundle of twigs. Tightly wound and full of strength, but with each worry and each uncertainty, the twigs unraveled. Bit by bit, they were thrown into a glowing flame. And yet, there was still a semblance of strength. I'd wake up, I'd show up, and I'd smile. I loved those babies of mine fiercely and only gave them the best of me.

My safe space became a dark corner in my closet. Shockingly, because I'm deathly afraid of the dark. And ghosts. And being in the dark with ghosts. Which is a great fear to have because kids see ghosts ALL THE TIME. At least my kids do. Do they make a bubble bath with sage?

Dave and I came to an unspoken agreement when it came to my time in the closest with the dark and the ghosts – when I needed it, I could go there to cry. Snot and tears would run down my face in unison. I'd gasp for air between screams and stutters. Into a pillow, of course. And then I'd hyperventilate my way through intrusive thoughts and anxieties. Surprisingly, none of them were about being in the dark with ghosts. I did this until I exhausted myself – until the only thing left was a somber sadness. Only then would I crawl out of my closet with puffy eyes, snotty sleeves, and a little bit of pee in my pants. Because whether I'm laughing or crying, there's always a little bit of dribble.

I think a switch went off when my dad almost died – I learned my panic wouldn't have saved him. Panic doesn't do any good in an emergency situation. And by the time Max arrived, I had been living life one emergency situation after the other. Except for this time, I was living through these emergencies as a mother. And these emergencies involved my babies.

A powerful strength comes over you when you have to protect your children. That instinct to protect is immediate, even if your bond with them is not. It's almost animalistic. You will speak up, you will stand against, and you will chastise any person or situation that puts them in harm's way. I've seen this instinct really come to fruition in specific scenarios since becoming a mom. Like that time a four-year-old told my two-year-old his voice was weird. A trigger because my baby was a late talker and navigating speech therapy. *OH, YEAH?* I thought. *Well, your Paw Patrol shirt is STUPID.* I had a week's worth of shower fight content because a kid thought it was funny that my toddler said "dick" instead of "stick." This instinct was also strong in both of my pregnancies – I had to keep my babies safe. They lived inside of me; therefore, the responsibility to keep them safe was solely mine.

When my sweet babies were earthside, they were welcomed by an entire team of overprotective aunts, uncles, and grandparents at their every beck and call. And I think because of that, I allowed myself to unravel. And the only person who knew was Dave.

Here was a relatively new father. A bad boy turned

husband turned dad of two kids under two. He was learning to change diapers and mix bottles while also trying to figure out what the hell a peepee teepee was. It was like he snapped his fingers and went from a fearless and fun 27-year-old guy to a 28-year-old man who was trying to grasp onto what it meant to be a parent – what it meant to be married and be a parent, what it meant to be an employee and be a parent, what it meant to be a son and be a parent, what it meant to be a human and be parent, and he while navigating all of that, his wife was slipping away. The parachute wouldn't open.

Max was born at the beginning of 2018, and in June 2018, the world was shocked when fashion designer and entrepreneur Kate Spade took her life. The news of Kate's death spread like wildfire on social media. After all, she was young, a doting mother, in otherwise good health, and thought to be one-half of a happy, successful marriage. Any personal struggles of Kate's seemed unbeknownst to her inner circle of close friends, family, and colleagues, as well as fans and patrons of the namesake brand she pulled up by the bootstraps. Kate Spade and her untimely death became my backup parachute – she saved my life just before I hit the ground.

How could it be? How could someone go from quietly fighting their demons (unbeknownst to anyone around them) one minute to taking their life the next? Did she get to a point where she completely lacked control? Because if she did, I felt like I was close. Kate's death rocked me. I was young. I was a doting mother. I loved my children and my husband fiercely – but my goodness, I almost thought they would be better off without me.

19

MEDS SAVE LIVES (MINE IN PARTICULAR)

The first time I took an antidepressant felt exactly like the first time I gave my baby a bottle of formula. A torrent of shame rushed over my body; my stomach was filled with knots. It's what I imagine lactose intolerance feels like after sneaking a piece of cheese. Explosive. Yes, that's exactly the word for it, the anxiety was explosive. Worst-case scenarios flooded my thoughts. Something in my intestines started a war. An uneasiness overcame every inch of my body. It was time to admit that my mental health had grown beyond something I could manage without tried-and-true medical support.

Standing in my kitchen, barefoot, with the cold tile below, I slowly twisted off the cap on the orange prescription bottle, just as I had slowly pulled back the lid of the formula months earlier. With hesitation. Dainty and white, what lay within would be my first step toward healing. And while these pivotal moments in my life came in different forms, one was a pill, and one was powder – both had a purpose larger than I could understand at the time.

Standing in Dave's arms, I examined the pill, running my fingers over the tiny grooves as tears filled my eyes. This was one of those moments where I knew there was no going back. Like death or the ultimate betrayal, there was now going to be a line in my life – before and after meds.

Tears crept down my cheeks as I placed the pill on my tongue. There was not one single person I knew on antidepressants, let alone anyone who had battled perinatal and postpartum depression. I was floating out to sea all on my own with a tiny white pill as my life raft. My only hope was that the raft would draw the attention of a rescue boat and bring me safely back to shore. Except, this raft did me dirty. This raft was like a Jack and Rose situation via the Titanic. I was Jack. My med was Rose. We wanted to work together. We wanted to get safely back to land. Except my body didn't react well to the medication. My luck, right? I had a rare and adverse reaction causing me extreme episodes of panic. I wanted to crawl out of my skin. I sat in the corner of my bedroom, rocking with my head between my knees. Diving into a deeper place than I had been before medication. And after a week of insomnia, panic, and even lower lows, I threw my pills into the garbage. Like Jack, I let go of the raft and drifted to the bottom of the sea.

The thing with this whole Jack and Rose metaphor is that in real life, Jack died. He sacrificed himself so Rose could stay out of the water and stay safe. He gave Rose an opportunity to live. And believe it or not – throwing my pills in the garbage did the exact same thing for me. It gave me a chance to live. It led me in a different direction – from 20 mg of Zoloft to 10 mg of Cipralex. And Cipralex was the life raft that brought me safely back to shore.

If a phoenix truly rises from the ashes, this would be

when my rise began. Would it be graceful? Heck no. You've read this far – everything about my life comes with some sort of mess. I'd stumble and fall along the way. I'd sob and cry like Kim Kardashian when she lost her diamond earring in the Tahitian ocean. There would be good days, and there'd be bad days and I'd have to figure out a new dose and carry on. I'd experience shame. I'd experience pride. I'd often feel like I was on my own island all alone. But I'd push through the ups and downs. I'd come to terms with my depression. I'd go on to live.

The important thing to know about medication is that it's not one size fits all. Not every medication works for every person. It can bring relief, but there isn't one solution to treating depression or mental health. It's not something you take once in a while when you're having a bad day. Medication is used as a treatment method for people with postpartum depression, anxiety, or mental illness. Often used as a last resort when all other options have been exhausted. This shouldn't discourage you from trying medication as a form of treatment, and if anything, it should encourage you to pay attention to what's working for you.

People who rely on medication to treat their mental health are people just like me. They don't have a character flaw, they're not empty – they're sick. Mental illness is not a choice, it's an illness. But thankfully, like people with diabetes have insulin, we have SSRIs – and those pills save lives. Sometimes, they save marriages and childhoods, too. They can help lift someone out of a pit of dark emotions and support them in functioning day to day. Medication helps filter the logical thoughts from the irrational. They regulate chemical imbalances in the brain that cause chaotic and anxious thoughts. And did I mention that they save lives? Because they save lives.

Medication is not the easy way out. It won't leave you dancing in the street, beaming with excitement, or cha-cha sliding over a rainbow. Although, a good cha-cha slide has never dampened anyone's spirit. Medication also won't change your circumstances. The things that were hurting and overwhelming you will still be there.

Sometimes treating mental health requires medication **and** therapy. Or medication **and** yoga. Or medication **and** deliciously decadent chocolate ice cream. Even with my medication, I still feel sad and overwhelmed. Those feelings make me human. Except now, maybe they put me in bed for a few hours rather than days.

It's true. Sadness and overwhelm still rear their ugly head from time to time. It usually happens when I've forgotten to take care of myself. Because meds and solely meds aren't the only piece of the treatment puzzle. Self-love and self-care go a long way too. Medication doesn't make you invincible. And at the end of the day, feelings send us an important message. The brilliant thing about medicine is that it gives us the awareness to navigate those feelings before they put us in a dark place.

Muhammad Ali once said, "Some mountains are higher than others. Some roads are steeper than the next. There are hardships and setbacks, but you cannot let them stop you. Even on the steepest road, you must not turn back." When I continued searching for the right pill, I committed to myself and my family to heal – to get better, to introduce my children to the real me. Heck, I wanted to *be* the real me once again. It had been so long since I saw her last, so many years ago. It was before young love and various groups of friends. Before eyeshadows and razor blades, and salon chairs. The last time I saw her was when I was just a little girl filled with life and dreams. She smelled of strawberry Lip Smackers and warm vanilla mist. I was filled with authenticity. Just like my kids are now – the purest versions of themselves.

And I guess that's just one of the many things I love about being a mom. That's just one of the many ways they inspired my soul to return home. I get to experience my kids' full throttle. For now, at least, I get them all in. I get them at one in the morning with cheeky smiles and gazing eyes. I get them at two in the afternoon with big angry feelings and pouty lips. I get the best and the worst of them, and everything in between. No one sees my kids the way I do. They don't see them fearlessly shaking what their mama gave them. They don't see them one, two, or three times a night looking for a safe place to rest their head. They don't see them taking those first shaky steps or fixing their hair for their first date. They don't see their joy, excitement, love, anger, frustration, or zest for life the way I do. My babies are unapologetically themselves in every way. When Jack grows up, he wants to be an "Engineer Fisherman." Max wants to be a "Builder Man," and I think – if I string the sounds together – Abby wants to be Peppa Pig. They don't overthink it. They're in it to live their best life.

As my babies grow, the world will want them to learn to manage their emotions – the big ones and the small ones – the way it did to us. The world will ask them to be humble and loyal and quiet while also encouraging them to look and act a certain way. And I guess that's why I'm here, trying to figure out where it all went wrong. Trying to understand what it was about certain influences that made me drift away. Because I was authentic once. I danced, I laughed, I lived authentically – and then the world made me quiet.

There is a joy in my babies' eyes that I never want to see fade. It's there on Christmas mornings, the moments we dance effortlessly in our kitchen, in their most vulnerable moments tucked between their dad and me on the couch. They enjoy the simplest things. Family is of the utmost importance. Love comes easy. Blippi is King. I'm learning little life lessons through their eyes, and it's shaken me awake. Their authenticity has reminded me of who I once was. My children's innocence, their awe, their wonder... their zero-fucks-given approach to life, it makes me feel alive (also so fucking tired, but alive). Motherhood is not the reason I'm lost. In fact, it steered me in the direction of freedom.

20

YOUR VOICE IS ONLY ONE THAT MATTERS (UNLESS ANOTHER VOICE IS OFFERING CAKE)

It's easy to get swept up in the beliefs of the people you look to for guidance. Especially if those beliefs are associated with fear. For example, there is my deeply embedded (and very real) belief in ghosts. A result of my dad's ghost stories, I'm sure. The result: I'm a 32-year-old woman who can't watch Casper while I'm home alone. Truthfully, I simply can't be home alone, period. I need a grownup with me at all times.

Author's note: In an effort to convince you just how scary my dad's ghost stories are, I went down a Google rabbit hole of the most terrifying ghost stories in the world. Then I sifted through a few examples, hoping to really drive the point home. But the title of an article scared the crap out of me, and I had to close my computer. Dave just finished clearing my browser history – I'm writing the rest of this book by the glow of my laptop under my covers.

My dad. The man tells a wicked ghost story. He's also had first-hand experiences with ghosts.

As have I.

Which he can validate.

Somebody get us a TLC show.

Now, it's not all his fault, because I also buy into crystals, read the obituaries, and speak to my spirit guides. No one else in my family does this. I'm just wired this way… I'm obsessed with the spiritual realm. I'm also a big believer in superstitions. I don't walk under ladders, I throw salt over my shoulder, and I never step on sidewalk cracks. That's a lie. I stepped on a sidewalk crack once, then immediately recited the classic children's rhyme, "Step on a crack, and you'll break your mother's back." Panicked, I called my mom and told her to sit the heck down as I rummaged through a stranger's lawn hunting for a four-leaf clover. It took a while, and I was mistaken for a landscaper, but I found one.

Thankfully, I'm better prepared these days. I carry around a lucky rabbit's foot and a pocket full of crystals at all times – should a superstitious emergency arise.

It's funny how that works, isn't it? The way we adopt beliefs, mannerisms, and behaviours, from our parents and the people who raised us. It's like osmosis.

Over the years, I've picked up a handful of quirks from my mom and dad. But before I throw stones from a glass house, I should be completely transparent that my five-year-old swears like a sailor. Yesterday he muttered, "For fucks sake," as he watched his sister throw yoghurt from her highchair onto the floor. I don't want to pat myself on the back or anything, but he picked that up from me.

Parents try really hard to do their very best. But sometimes, we slip up. Sometimes our fears and irrationalities (and let's not forget, good qualities, too) rub off on our kids. We are the total sum of our life experiences, and parents influence our development in the most prominent way.

I've picked up some *really* interesting mannerisms from my parents. Sandwiches were called "sangwiges" in my house when I was growing up – and that's carried forward into my life today. I also do the sign of the cross any time I pass by a cemetery as a sign of respect for the dead. My mom used to discreetly mark them on her forehead during rides in the car. There are other things about my mom that stand out. Like how she casually adds an "S" to the end words that shouldn't have them, like Costcos and LaSenzas. But I think that's a phenomenon that comes with age.

Anyway – where was I? Oh yes, the beautiful traits we pick up from our families. Fears and traumas can pass from one generation to another. Just as our positive traits do: generosity, compassion, empathy, understanding…an authentic way of living that makes you feel like a badass bitch.

This is why recovery is so important to me. While my kids may very well end up believing in ghosts, I don't want them to pick up any of the negative traits associated with my anxiety or depression. Like crawling into your bed for the entire day anytime, someone makes even the slightest criticism against you. Or saying something incredibly awkward and inappropriate during a social gathering. Sometimes, I wonder if my recovery started just a little too late. My kids have big feelings, and I'm not beyond blaming myself for them. Did they feel enough love when they were babies? Could they sense how overwhelmed I was? Did they know they were my everything despite everything I was feeling and struggling with? I'll never know because they were too little to ever communicate it with me. And while I tried my damnedest to protect them from my struggles, I'll never know for sure if any damage was done.

I want them to be able to connect and identify with their feelings – both big and small. But I want their feelings to be simply that...theirs.

I want to understand the depths of my trauma, dissect the various influences over the course of my life, and dust off the foundation of my being so that I can live a happier, more fulfilling life. I've come to believe that my struggles with mental health started long before I ever had babies. There was a crack in my mental well-being caused by the years of adapting and pivoting and trying to please. Failed relationships and peers, tabloids, and media. They influenced me more than I ever had influence over myself. I lost my sparkle – my raw and unapologetic zest for life. I completely forgot it even existed until I saw my kids' zero-fucks-given approach to getting what they want. I completely forgot what it was like to scream and cry for what I believed in until I told my toddler, "no." Now, if we threw it down in Nordstrom the way my kids throw it down in Toys R Us, we'd get arrested. But there's something about the way kids fight for things that they want, that we lose as we grow up. And instead of going after what feels right, we become people who try to obtain more of what we don't need.

For a long time, I believed more is more. More friends meant I was more likable. More money meant I was more valuable. More attention meant I was more desirable. But after living a life chasing more, I've come to realize only one thing: more is bullshit when the quality of what you have is crap. What you truly need in your life are people, places, and things that serve you in your most authentic state and make you feel good. Releasing anything unworthy of your attention is your first step towards a truly abundant life. This means people, places, or things who don't serve you can see the door. It's kind of like a full Marie Kondo on your life. Does your friend Sally bring you joy? No? Then bye-bye, Sally. You're a mom now. You don't owe anything to anyone (except the little people within your home). And most of all, you don't have the time or energy for anything with a low vibe.

Truth be told, kids can have a pretty low vibe. Especially toddlers. Specifically, age three, but who's holding a grudge? My kids have literally asked me to make them macaroni and cheese for dinner, only to tell me I'm the "worst mommy ever" for making macaroni and cheese for dinner. Those are some low freaking vibes. Unfortunately, when those low vibes bubble to the surface, we can't kick them to the curb. We have to learn to take those low vibes in stride. Dirt off the shoulder, if you will. Everyone else, though, can take their low vibes and go.

You owe it to yourself to heal and overcome the untrue things people have projected onto you. It is time to dig into the truths that lie within. Quite honestly, if you haven't healed from hurt from previous relationships or if those people are still active in your life, you will never value yourself the way you deserve. Every time you feel an ounce of doubt in yourself (especially as a mother, because we tend to doubt ourselves a lot), those embedded insecurities will take charge.

We have a paper trail of insecurities that can be tied back to people we have met in our life. Some of these people have just happened to be people we met in passing, while others have been people that we truly love and trust. Unfortunately, the words and actions of the people we love seem to stick with us the longest. The same can be said for significant moments – such as bullying or targeted events causing trauma.

I want you to say this with me – you are more than your insecurities. I know I said this book wasn't about convincing you to be, do, or have more, but if I'm going to fall back on my word anywhere, it's here. You deserve to be more aligned with your higher self, you deserve to do more of what feels good, and you deserve to have a more authentic life.

The first time I truly tuned into the idea of overcoming my insecurities was when I was twenty-one. The most significant relationship of my life had just ended. Looking back now, that relationship was all phooey. The love was phooey. All of it was so juvenile and phooey. It also all had its place and purpose in my life – to develop an understanding of my worth. It wasn't until I cultivated this understanding that I'd meet my husband, Dave.

When I first met my husband, my best friend at the time told me he wasn't good for me, though my gut knew differently. She tried to steer me away from giving this new man a chance. To this day, it's never been clear why. She was like a sister to me; her family was my family. I trusted her opinion on everything – except her opinion on my new man. Dating in my early twenties was different from when I was dating when I was in my teens. I wasn't looking for anyone's approval when it came to my partner. At least not right away, which was new to me. Usually, I wanted my entire gang of girls to weigh in. Was he cute enough? Fun enough? Did my friends like him enough? But after getting out of a bad relationship with a fun, cute guy my friends liked a ton, I realized it wasn't their validation that I needed. I needed to listen to my intuition.

In my prior relationship, my intuition was drowned out by manipulation. I mean, it was still there. It was still whispering, I heard the whispers, but I pushed that voice down and ignored everything it was trying to say. I was in love, and I was determined to make the relationship work – even though it was hurting me. That relationship lasted four years – and none of my friends, especially my best friend, tried to talk me out of it.

When Dave came into my life, though, a lot had changed. I had entered a new chapter and a new fresh start. Determined to avoid my past mistakes, I chose not to listen to the guidance of my friend and instead tuned into my intuition. In going through my previous relationship, I learned a lot about myself. Then, when that relationship ended, I had a decision: Would I listen to others, or would I listen to the voice coming from inside? I don't know why I chose to listen to my internal voice. To be honest, I've gone most of my life looking for reassurance from others. I still crave reassurance from my husband – but the way he talks me through my insecurities and uncertainties only helps me better connect with myself.

When my best friend tried to steer me away from my gut, I stood my ground. It was a risk I was willing to take on this new journey of listening to my own voice. The voice that told me this man was mine to have. My best friend, on the other hand, drifted away. About a year later, our relationship hit a fork in the road, and this girl who was once my sister is now a stranger. That young man that she told me to run from, is now my husband and the absolute love of my life. Heaven knows where I would be today if I had chosen to listen to a voice louder than my own.

Listening to your own voice is one of the greatest gifts you can give yourself. The soft voice is usually kind, offering encouraging words of wisdom that nags you until you listen. They may encourage you to hold yourself to a higher standard or chase a dream. Your soft voice isn't dark, hurtful, or discouraging. It provides direction or redirection in a positive light. It's taken a lot of work for me to learn the difference between my own voice and the voice of insecurity. I've learned that negative self-talk directly results from psychological issues such as aggression or post-traumatic stress disorder. It's not your words; it's *theirs, w*hile your authentic inner voice comes from your heart. Some even think the inner voice is a whisper from God. Wherever the voice comes from, it's here to drive your life toward your purpose. The first time I truly tuned into my inner voice, it brought me a man who set the path forward for my future. The whispers brought me Dave. Dave gave me my babies – and my babies gave me an awakening I had been searching for my entire life.

My awakening is solely thanks to motherhood and thanks to listening to my inner voice. I wouldn't have woken up any other way. But that's my story. It might not be yours. You don't need to become a mother to uncover your truth. You don't need to become a mother to start living your most authentic life. You don't need to become a mother to have a purpose. But I did. I needed to become a mother to find myself. I needed to become a mother to understand my purpose. Just like I believe my postpartum depression had a purpose, and each of my children has a purpose, and every good, bad, ugly, and hard experience in my life has a purpose. Our experiences and the people we live with are all a part of who we are and who we will become. But, to grow into our most authentic selves, we must listen to the soft voice – otherwise, we'll continue to live a life that doesn't serve us. A life that doesn't make us feel complete.

My job as a parent is to teach my kids right from wrong and good from the bad. My job is to teach them patience – which is hard when you're raising them in a world of instant gratification. My job is to raise them to understand that life won't always go their way and to accept what comes with grace. But there's something about the absolute certainty they want for things that I hope they never lose.

If I pass anything on to my kids – besides my teenage angst and acne (sorry, babes)...and maybe my fear of ghosts – I hope I pass on everything I've learned from them. Because of them, I get excited when I see a giant fat worm after a spring rain. Because of them, I put extra sprinkles on my ice cream. Because of them, I dance in the grocery checkout line. Anything that's not worth my time doesn't get it – and it's all because of them. I hope how they've inspired me never gets lost on them. And I hope it inspires them in a roundabout way, too.

It's really funny how my life has all come together from when I first began writing this book, which was at the end of 2018. Just like me – this book has changed. It started with such a different premise. At the time, I had an interested agent who wanted me to rebrand myself as the "Millennial Mom." He wanted me to change the concept of my book – claim to be some type of millennial Mom expert – which I'm not...and I rolled with it. Another problem here is that he was a "he." He didn't fully grasp just how important *my* story was to me and why I wanted to tell it in my way. But just like the many times before, I strayed from my path. I let someone – who held power over me – tell me I needed to be someone different, and I listened.

You'll never hear that version of my book because I never finished it. Writing lost its spark, and I walked away from the idea of writing a book altogether – until each piece of who I am slowly found its way back.

My book and I hardly look the same as we did four years ago – because, at the time, I really didn't know who I was. What I was going to offer didn't have depth. My babies were still babies, and I had so much more to learn about motherhood and myself. The learning still isn't over – it never will be. But at least now, I can say I know who I am – and that's an excellent place to start.

It's easy to *think* you've lost your identity in sleepless nights, sweatpants, and goober. But there is a big difference between losing yourself and drifting astray. In the early parts of motherhood, I felt lost. I believed I was lost. And there is some truth in that. But I wasn't lost because I became a mom. Reflecting back, I confused the feeling of being lost with the feeling of being frustrated.

My body was different – curvier, wider, heavier… and I thought I felt lost because of it. But really, I was frustrated when clothes didn't fit my new curves. Or when something didn't fit me off the rack. Or when I couldn't get my favourite jeans over my thighs. Sometimes, I felt lost within the four walls of my home caring for my kids. But really, I was frustrated that my anxiety limited my ability to socialize and build friendships. And even then, good friends are hard to come by as an adult (especially a mom) – but that could be an entire book in itself.

Sometimes, I thought I felt lost in my marriage. My husband and I passed like two ships in the night (often, we still do). But really, I was frustrated because we weren't spending enough quality time together. And because my husband didn't have working boobs. What the eff, man? I also felt lost in my career and primarily used it to identify who I was – and in that sense, I was lost. I wasn't working in a career that I was passionate about. The idea of leaving my babies to return to a career that didn't fill my cup ate me up inside. I needed adult interaction and personal fulfillment outside of raising my beautiful children.

But if something was going to take me away from them – I needed to justify that it was something that would make me happy.

21

I ONLY TAKE PHOTOS FROM MY "GOOD SIDE"

Word on the street is that the most beautiful faces are symmetrical. Mine's not. I have a weird mole on the right side of my nose. It grows hairs, too. Not just one hair – hairs. Plural. This mole hasn't always been there, though. It appeared some time in my teens. And I remember its arrival because my mom treated it like a zit. She doused a cotton ball in tea tree oil and secured it with a Band-Aid. This golden (and very potent) super oil was supposed to make it disappear. It didn't. That sucker grew roots, and it stayed. Hairy Mole and I have been companions for about two decades now – time flies when you're having fun – and while I haven't grown to *love* the hairy mole on the side of my face, I've come to accept that it is what it is.

I like to think Hairy Mole has had a bigger purpose in my life. One destined to prepare me to accept that, yes – physical things about us can change. Parts of our body can become unfamiliar. But just because there's a little extra hair here or a little extra mole there, you're still the same old beautiful gal on the inside. I wish I had taken more time reflecting on that when Hairy Mole first came into my life instead of covering it with foundation, dousing it in tea tree oil, and literally trying to cut it off my face. I also wish I had spent some more time loving who I was on the inside, too. That certainly would have helped as my body underwent various changes through the decades. But eventually, Hairy Mole became a part of me. When I look in the mirror, I hardly see it. But on the days when I'm feeling down on myself and the way that I look, it's among the things I fixate on the most.

It's funny how that works, isn't it? One day we're looking in the mirror loving every damn piece about ourselves – and the next – ugh. *I hate that stupid hairy mole.* But time and aging, stress and cortisol, babies, and a pandemic change our bodies in an incredible way. Extra floof, extra fluff, extra skin. After three kids, my once perky and perfect boobs look like Ziploc bags filled with yogurt. My stomach – which was once smooth and firm – now rolls over itself with a bunch of extra skin. Things change. And when it came to having kids, I kind of expected it. I knew I'd get bigger and wider, though I hoped, like every model on every cover of every magazine, I'd quickly "bounce back." I bounce all right. I also knew what to expect when it came to getting older. Some gray hairs here, maybe a little extra weight there...I think there's a point where our height starts to shrink, too. But if I followed my grandmother's tried-and-true method, a thick slathering of Nivea cream before bed would save me from wrinkles until I was well into my sixties.

Yes, I expected some things would change. I just wasn't exactly prepared for how those physical changes would make me feel after babies (not to mention turning 30) – but with some self-work, I've eventually come around to bigger jeans and thinner hair. Do I still have sex with a shirt on and the lights off? Of course, I do. Acceptance is a process, and I'm taking it one new body quirk at a time.

Man, I took that early twenties body of mine for granted. I should have taken more nudes. Made a sex tape. Something to time capsule how tight and toned it all really was.

Just kidding. *Mom, you okay?*

But really, you don't know what you have until it's gone – or someone threatens to take it.

At nearly nine months pregnant with Max, just weeks away from delivery, I was sent for a routine ultrasound on my thyroid. My doctor was tracking the growth of a single nodule. Nothing major. Nothing to be worried about. We were keeping an eye on it…just in case.

I hoisted myself up and onto the exam table – my belly the size of a dump truck – and laid on my back. The ultrasound technician graciously helped me turn to my side as a fart snuck out. Silent but deadly. I remember the heavy weight of my baby pressing down on my bladder, counting the minutes until I could roll back to my feet and waddle to the bathroom. Time ticked by; the wand drifted from one side of my neck to the next. Over my thyroid, up and down, and back again. All done? Cool. Time to pee.

A few days later – right on schedule for how my life rolls – I received a phone call from my doctor. My nodule was great, unchanged. My parotid gland, however – *parotid what?* – it had something funky in it. It looked like a crystal – but it also could have been a growth. Whatever it was, I'd have to wait until after I had my baby to follow up with an MRI. This wasn't great news for a pregnant lady who was supposed to be managing her stress for the sake of her glitchy uterus.

Weeks later, just as planned, my middle little, Maxwell Richard, arrived curious and calm. He was everything I never knew I needed. Perfect in every way. But I couldn't get too comfortable in that newborn bliss. My parotid gland was coming in hot – and it was about to fuck shit up.

Weeks after my c-section, I found myself in another cold exam room, waiting on rare and unexpected medical results. I sat anxiously in the dentist-like exam chair with posters of nasal cavities plastered on the walls around me. A nurse came in to confirm my birthday. I stumbled over the date. August. My birthday was in August. Was that enough to go by? She smiled kindly because she had seen people like me before. An anxious patient waiting on life-changing news. August was enough.

Minutes behind her, a dashing and handsome ENT walked into the room. I adjusted myself in my seat and tucked my hair behind my ears. There was something about his confidence that made me feel safe. He sat across from me and smiled as he introduced himself and explained why I was there. Then he told me his wife just had a baby – only 17 months after their first. I knew for certain I was in good hands. Quickly, Dr. K understood my deepest fears, and thanks to our common ground as parents, he saw me as more than just a patient. He saw me as Jack and Max's mom.

As Dr. K sat across from me, looking at my chart, he validated my biggest fear – that I had a tumor embedded in my main salivary gland. A biopsy would later confirm it was benign-mixed. It wasn't cancer yet, but it needed to come out. Due to the size of the tumor and the proximity to my facial nerves, there was a chance I would have serious facial paralysis. To save my facial nerves, I would likely need radiation. My entire life – the completion of our family – our future…my future- flashed before my eyes.

That conversation flipped my world upside down. I was only twenty-eight. I was a young mom with a young family and a whole life ahead. I refused to be another near-miss statistic.

~

If there's anything you don't want to hear your surgeon say – it's that your surgery is so complicated that they don't want to do it. In fact, they're going to refer you to the top surgeon in the province – but don't worry, *you'll be in the best of hands.* My mind went to a thousand places. And you would think – since facial paralysis was one of my biggest risks – that I would be worried about what I looked like when all was said and done. But as I sat in that office, my beauty wasn't what I thought of. It was the idea of losing my ability to smile at my babies or kiss my husband as we fell asleep. I didn't worry about how I would look in the mirror or to the public and how I would fail to meet our regressive beauty standards. All that mattered at that moment was life.

I thought about my boys learning to ride a two-wheel bicycle or walking across the stage at graduation in a cap and gown. I thought about my husband sitting on the porch that was supposed to be ours, eyes with wrinkles where dark circles once were and gray running through his hair. I thought about all the Christmases that were to come. The broken hearts I wanted to help mend and the weddings I wanted to dance at. I thought about growing old, how my body was supposed to change, and how I wanted it all.

At age twenty-eight, a scar down the side of my neck wouldn't impact my beauty, a spot like that meant survival.

With two babies under two, a husband I adored, and a spunky puppy dog I loved just the same, a scar was the best possible outcome.

The fury bubbled and boiled. The rage surfaced and couldn't be contained. My body had let me down in both of my pregnancies, and now it was trying to take me away from my family. I lost my career, my sense of self, and my identity, and now, I met with the threat of losing my face – because if I kept it, I could lose my life.

I spent eight agonizing months waiting for my surgery date to arrive. I overanalyzed every what-if, trying to prepare myself for the worst while hoping for the best. I had never been under general anesthesia before – what if I died because of that? Should I record a video message for each of my babies' birthdays until they're eighteen? Should I write them a heartfelt letter to read on their wedding day? I had gone from intrusive and uncontrolled thoughts about death only months early – to begging and pleading to God for my life. I needed to watch my babies grow.

Eventually, the day came. I didn't prepare video birthday wishes or letters for their weddings. I went in with a promise to survive and never take my life or my face for granted again. I remember standing in front of the mirror, looking at my face one last time. Smiling. Puckering my lips. Taking it all in…the girl in the mirror. The girl I cursed so many times, for she never reflected beauty or success or anything she dreamed of being. At least not in my eyes. My face was the only thing on my body that looked familiar since becoming a mother, despite a few wrinkles and dark circles, of course. It was the only time in my life that my face made me feel safe.

Now, it was time to say goodbye.

I thanked the girl in the mirror. I know she felt weak at that moment. I know she felt like she had hardly been getting by for the last two years – but she was strong. I thanked her, and I told her this was where things were going to change. From this point forward – she was going to live.

Dave held my hand in the car, though we spoke no words. There was nothing we could say. I was afraid. He was calm. It was typical of us. He held my hand as we parked, as we walked, and as I lay on the table about to go under the knife.

The bright lights beamed down on me as the anesthesiologist administered medication, and I counted back from ten. Everything went black. Laying in that state of darkness, with my life in someone else's hands, the surgeon cut a six-inch incision from the top of my ear and down the side of my neck. Hours later, the entire tumor had been removed. I wouldn't need radiation; a third baby was still a possibility.

Eventually, I woke up, and sleepy and confused, I smiled. I still had my face.

22

SO WHAT? THINGS COULD BE WORSE

I'm going to pre-empt this with a trigger warning for anyone who was a teen in the early 2000s. In fact, the following few sentences might stir up some buried feelings. You may even feel inclined to dig out your old Sony Walkman, pop in a Good Charlotte C.D, and track down your MySpace page. Don't say I didn't warn you because here it goes:

I was the girl who wore Von Dutch hats and popped collars. I also wore bubble dresses with wide braided belts and a choker necklace. Trust me; this hurts me more than it hurts you.

I feel like I should stop, but I will keep going down this tacky path.

Livestrong bracelets, butterfly clips, chunky highlights, flat ironed hair (with a literal clothing iron), side parts (which I'm honestly still on board with), blue eyeshadow, colorful eyeliner, frosted lip gloss – and I've said it once. Still, I'll say it again: overplucked, ultra-thin eyebrows. Whew, that's giving me some strong Tara Reid vibes circa

2002.

I don't know about you, but I was "that" for basically
a third of my life. As for the other two-thirds, nineties
fashion recently made a comeback – so I've spent roughly
66 percent of my life in loose-fitting jeans, chunky
sneakers, and graphic tees.

My sense of self has ebbed and flowed with each and
every fashion trend and beauty statement. And as I've
ebbed and flowed, I've grown more comfortable in my own
skin. But I wouldn't be honest if I said I love every bit of
myself today. Based on the whole tumor thing – you think
that I would. You'd think that I learned one of life's hardest
lessons, and it shook me awake. But I still look in the
mirror and pick myself apart. I see lines and wrinkles and
extra skin. I'm not always easy on myself.

The good news is that my self-criticism has evolved.
These days, it comes with two different feelings:
acceptance and guilt.

Here's how acceptance works: I've accepted that I
like how pizza tastes, and I hate anything that feels like
exercise. I've also accepted that I haven't slept in six years,
so I *should* look like someone who hasn't slept in six years.
When my pants feel just a little too tight, I've accepted it's
because I haven't tried to keep off any extra weight. When
the black circles under my eyes hang down to the floor,
I've accepted it's because I don't prioritize the little sleep
I do have. It's a work in progress, but I try to accept that
I am a reflection of my current sleepless and fast-paced
environment. With that being said, I also experience a lot
more guilt than I ever have before when I'm feeling down
on myself about the parts of myself I've "accepted."

Not only do I know firsthand that things could be much worse, but I've lived it and survived it. Three separate times I've landed on the lucky side of the statistic. So, each and every time I criticize a piece of my physical body or curse motherhood under my breath, I also yell at myself for taking my life for granted. I feel an overwhelming guilt that things could have been so much worse. My mind flashes back and recounts the painful moments I've endured over the last few years. It's like an out-of-body experience. I see myself in each cold doctor's office receiving each piece of heart-wrenching news. I relive every time I prayed at the foot of my bed or in the car to or from an appointment. I relive the moment I was lying on an operating table, praying to God to wake up with my face. I promised to love myself and know my worth. I promised to always be grateful for what I had. Just please, God, please…let me wake up with my face. And my prayers were answered.

I relive the moment early in my first pregnancy when the amniocentesis needle went into my belly. I relive the ambulance ride during my second pregnancy when I was in threatened preterm labour. Please let my baby be healthy; please give them a chance at life. I'll always be grateful; I'll never take them for granted. Just please, God, please… answer my prayers. And my prayers were answered.

Since my surgery and since my pregnancies, and since those dire times of need, I've taken my face for granted, I've wanted time away from my kids. I've thought about getting Botox and plastic surgery. I've complained that motherhood is hard (heck, I kind of wrote a book about it…). I've thought about myself and my life in ways I promised myself I wouldn't. And I feel so much guilt about it.

But here's where it circles back to acceptance and

learning to let go. Here is what I really believe: just because the road was hard, just because we promised ourselves (and God and the universe and whoever the hell would listen) that we'd always be grateful in exchange for an answered prayer, does it mean we have to love everything in every moment all the time? Because honestly, I find it hard. Despite what it took to get here.

I know I'm not the only one who struggles with guilt, and acceptance and gratitude all rolled into one. I've heard about this specific inner turmoil from parents who struggled with infertility. The parents who went through years of IVF and multiple losses just to get their one miracle baby. They feel like they need to zip it – push every contradicting emotion deep down inside – be grateful that they got their one.

Parents aren't allowed to complain – you signed up for it. Parents aren't allowed to complain – you're lucky you have a baby, to begin with. Simply, parents aren't allowed to complain. If we're not allowed to complain, can we call it something else then? Like reaching out for help... or looking for support...or expressing human emotion? Because that's actually what's happening. Are we grateful for our lives? Most of the time. We've all wondered what our beach house would look like in our alternative child-free life.

You can be grateful while also having ungrateful thoughts from time to time. I'm grateful I can smile – but I'm only human for getting down on myself from time to time. I'm beyond grateful I have my children – but dammit, parenting has its hard moments. I'm grateful for my life – but that doesn't mean I have to love every minute. Especially that time, one of my kids puked in the car. Which caused my other kid to puke in the car. Which caused me to puke in the car. A fundamental core memory in the making – but did I love it at the time? Abso-pukely not.

Motherhood comes with a lot of guilt – and I think one of the heavier weights we carry is that we should just be happy with what we have. Mothers should be happy they got their answered prayer. But gratefulness isn't the end all be all. Should it be practiced? Of course. Gratitude is scientifically proven to be a foundation for a happier life. But gratefulness doesn't trump those moments you need to feel – because, in the end, the feeling is what truly allows us to grow.

So, here's your permission – and it's only from me, so take it as you will – but you are allowed to be frustrated with your circumstances. You're allowed to vent when life gets hard and ask for support when you need it most. Being a parent doesn't mean you're not human. Everyone, from time to time, needs a little vent session. *Unless you're a parent, then you signed up for this.* Bologna. If we talk more openly about the less-than-stellar moments of parenting, I think we're actually kind of heroes in the making. Saving future parents from being misled the same way we were. Choosing to have kids doesn't give us complete control. I learned that after having one baby, and yet, I still went on to have two more. It was the right journey for me, even though getting there wasn't anything I expected.

Parents, we can simultaneously adore our children and hate that they've never slept longer than 45-minutes in their entire life. It's why we flip through 600 photos of them the minute they fall fast asleep. It's a love you can only understand when you join this exclusive club. So vent, complain, love hard, be prideful, feel grateful, and mutter a few *what the fucks* every now and then. It's normal. Or it's not, and I'm just a big complainer.

23

DON'T BLAME ME FOR MONKEY POX

A quick recap: baby number one – genetic scare, amniocentesis, the child who never slept. Baby number two: perinatal depression, threatened preterm labour, freak facial tumor. So, it would only make sense that baby number three would be conceived only months before a global pandemic. I hate to be the one to say it, but I may have been the cause of COVID-19. My pregnancies haven't exactly earned a reputation for being easy, breezy, beautiful. But if that's the case, you should be able to rest easily at night because Dave had a vasectomy two months after our last baby was born. Though, I should probably mention: that not one but TWO psychics recently told me we'd be having a spontaneous miracle baby in 2023. Come to think of it, the United Kingdom just declared a new outbreak…Monkey Pox. I should probably buy a pregnancy test.

Even after everything we had been through, Dave and I still wanted another baby. We like living life on the edge. But the truth is, our hearts felt like someone was missing. While our home was full, it wasn't full enough. We loved our boys – and if our family ended up just being the two of us and the two of them, we would have considered ourselves blessed beyond anything we deserved.

With that being said, people had opinions about us having a third baby. They especially had concerns about my postpartum depression – a valid point. But here's the thing: just because I had postpartum depression doesn't mean I don't love being a mom. Just because my road to motherhood wasn't easy doesn't mean raising children hasn't been my life's greatest pleasure.

My children are the reason I breathe. They're also the reason I cry, and binge eat cake – but they're my reason for being. They're the reason I sought help for a mental illness I lived with for years before their existence. They're the reason I wake up every day and push myself to be better. My children are the reason I found myself. The boogers on my walls and the bags under my eyes are worth it because I get to have them.

Having babies exposed me to a world I didn't know existed. And since becoming a mom, I've found more reasons to love and laugh and advocate for change.

When it came to planning our last baby, I thought we had finally had it figured out. I had journaled, prayed, meditated, and medicated to get myself to a good place. I even reached out to my most trusted and reputable sources: Facebook Mom Groups. The go-to for rashes, fevers, what's open and closed on holidays, and most importantly - the pros and cons of having more children. And when I asked them about the pros and cons of having a third baby, they laid it all out. And quite honestly, they scared the crap out of me. For one, surveys show that three kids is the most stressful number of kids to have. Another reason, parents of three are officially outnumbered – which didn't really matter to me because as a stay-at-home mom of two, I was outnumbered anyway. The consensus was that people love their kids, but three kids are *a lot* of kids.

We did it anyway. Dave and I went in for it and decided to finish our family with our third kid in under four years.

I've been a mom of three for a few years now. Not long enough to have an honest opinion, but long enough to have establish a bit of a rhyme and reason, and I can tell you this:

Having one kid was hard. Having two kids was hard. Having three kids is hard. In summary: having children is hard. For one, you never know who you're going to get. When you choose to grow your family, you have to be okay with the possibility of *anything*. For example, if you're a parent of two children of the same sex and you're "going for the boy/girl," you have to be okay with not getting what you want. Think long and hard about it because gender disappointment is a real thing.

Our third child ended up being a baby girl – and I'd be lying if I didn't say it was a dream come true. But I knew I had to be okay with having another penis in my house. Other boy moms look at our family with hope when we're out in public. But the thing is – you never know who you're going to get or who they'll grow up to be and what challenges they (and you) will face along the way. You have to be ready for *anything* and *everything*.

When people ask me what it's like having three kids and whether it's hard, my answer is: parenting is hard. It's all circumstantial, and the only circumstances you know and can attest to are your very own. You can't look at another person, family, or mom and think you can do it because she can. For one, she could barely be holding it together on her side of the fence. And two, are you ready to take on more within your own house and life? Will your marriage, mental health, and financial situation be okay with any and all outcomes? Because when you're adding to your family, you're not just adding a chunky little peanut to love on. You're adding a human being with quirks and needs who may or may not ever sleep through the night.

By the way, can we stop telling new parents their baby needs to sleep through the night? Telling parents their baby will sleep through the night with some random ritual that worked for you is setting them up for complete and utter failure. I see it all the time on Facebook. When will my baby sleep through the night? My four-month-old still has a night feed, when can I wean them? How do I get my twelve-week-old to stop waking up? Then people show up in groves sharing all kinds of advice – and I may be out of line here, but I think it's all crap.

I'm really passionate about the sleep thing, people. I used to ask those questions, too. I used to Google all of the things that could have possibly been wrong with my child because he wouldn't sleep. You know my postpartum depression? It stemmed from some of that, too. Not just because my baby wouldn't sleep, but because everyone and their mother were telling me I was doing something wrong. So, I obsessed with sleep, I read every blog and tried every method. Co-sleep, don't co-sleep. Sleep train, don't sleep train. Soother, no soother. Night feed, no night feed. Oh, holy night. I confused my poor baby (and myself) and made it worse for the both of us.

Peter Fleming, professor of infant health and development psychology at the University of Bristol, says the idea that babies should sleep through the night

is a 21st-century thing. It's natural for them to wake up…
often. Adults don't sleep through the night, either. Does
your baby want to be held? Hold them. Do they like their
soother? Buy a thousand and throw them around their crib.
Is your kid a magical unicorn who actually sleeps through
the night? Amazing. Don't step foot in their room; they'll
smell you and immediately wake up.

Parenting, friends. It's all easier said than done. There
truly is never a perfect time to have a baby. And sometimes,
another baby just *happens*. Sometimes people become
parents when it isn't *exactly* what their future had planned.
And that's why it's so important to ask for what we need
and talk about what's hard.

When I bared all about my genetic testing during my first
pregnancy, no one came out of the woodwork. I navigated
that bad boy all on my own. Sure, I found some strangers
on the internet to connect with, and they were great. But
there wasn't anyone physical I could hug or cry on that
truly got it. Then Jack came, and I continued with life. Next
came my preterm labour with Max. And my tumor. And my
postpartum depression. And my messy house. And hiring
someone to wash my laundry and put away my underwear
(hands down, the best gift I've ever given myself) – and I
blogged about it on my corner of the internet, where friends
and family and a growing number of followers read on the
sidelines.

The more I talked about our beautiful and imperfect
life; the more people showed up to do just the same. I
went from not having a safe space to reach out for help to
creating a safe space for others to do exactly that. Because
here's the thing – it takes a village. But the village doesn't
work unless you say "yes." As much as the village can see
you struggling and exhausted and deserving of a nap, they

can't force their way into your home. They can't force you to say, "I need help." For many moms, asking for help is hard, but look at it this way: the help isn't only for you, the help has benefits for you, your children, *and* your relationships.

I had long been the person who couldn't ask for help, and the thought of the village exhausted me. If someone offered to come over to clean my kitchen, I'd be on my hands and knees scrubbing the floors before they came. If someone offered to bring me a few homecooked meals to get through the week, I'd whip up a batch of muffins as a thank you. My need to please other people instead of just accepting their help left me anxiously turning away kind gestures (that really could have helped). But here's the thing – the village doesn't care. The village is there for YOU. The village gets it.

Now is not the time to be prideful. It's not the time to be ashamed of the bags under your eyes or the crumbs on your floor. The village doesn't care. Now is the time to say, "can you help me" and "I need you." You can even say, "This is harder than I ever thought it would be." The village is safe. We're all in this together. We have the power to bring back the village.

24

"JUST WAIT" *INSERT EYEROLL*

Do you remember what you wanted to be when you grew up? The age-old question where the sky is the limit. Especially as a child – because with magic and make-believe, anything is possible. When I was around my daughter's age, I wanted to be a ballerina or a princess… maybe even a dog. I really liked dogs. So, when Jack was 2-years-old, and I asked him what he wanted to be when he grew up, I fully expected something along the lines of a T-Rex or astronaut. His world revolved around dinosaurs and space at that age. Every day he imagined himself in one of those roles. He'd roar and stomp around our home with his dinosaur backpack on. He'd get his toy rocket ship ready for a trip to the moon. But when I asked him what he wanted to be when he grew up, he looked at me like I had three heads and answered me very matter-of-factly, "me be Jack." While he may not have understood the power of his answer, it completely stopped me in my tracks. My baby, wise beyond his years, wanted nothing more than to be himself.

It made me stop and think. Whichever profession or role we have in our life –whether it be a mother, doctor, teacher, ballerina, or an astronaut– it does not define who we are; it's simply something we do. Having a well-known job may sound great on a resume or impressive to a group of friends, but the only true definition of success is doing something you really love. And even then, life is full of uncertainties. A job is always temporary; employees can be replaced. People, on the other hand, cannot be replaced. Jack can never be replaced. Just like you and I can never be replaced. At the end of our life, we won't be remembered by our job – we will be remembered for how we made people feel, our personality, and our chapter. Those are the qualities that makeup who we are and, in turn, make us unforgettable to the people who cross our path in life.

I pray my kids never lose sight of who they are. I pray the world doesn't eat them up and spit them out, telling them they need to be someone they're not. I pray they never lose confidence in themselves. There were so many times I wanted to be someone else over the course of my life. Many times, I wanted to be someone I wasn't. And as much as I talk about how hard motherhood is, this is exactly where I am supposed to be.

I love that at thirty-two years old, I have three reasons to let my run spirit free. In the winter, I have three reasons to jump in piles of snow. When the wind picks up, I have three reasons to grab a kite and fly it in the breeze. I get to blow belly raspberries and sing along to Cocomelon in the car. While motherhood has its moments where I'm met with absolute defeat, it's reunited me with the things that are wonderful in this life. Love, laughter…stopping to literally smell the roses. The things that require us to slow down. And yet, when you're embedded in the world of motherhood, slowing down seems almost impossible.

When I reflect on my childhood, I remember the hours

my parents spent with me and my brother and jumping in piles of leaves. I remember hiking beautiful trails and splashing in the lake. I don't remember the time and energy my mom put into making our house a home, but it always seemed perfect to me. I don't remember the 70-hour weeks my dad spent at work, running his body into the ground – but I remember him playing hockey with us on the weekends and taking us sledding at dusk.

The moments I remember are the moments when my parents slowed down – and what beautiful moments those were. As my children get older, get busier, and need me a little less, I'm learning that, eventually the laundry gets put away. Eventually, the dishes in the sink (or in the dishwasher or on the counter) get washed. And while I'm still frantically trying to figure this whole thing out, I've hit that turning point in motherhood where you learn that nothing lasts forever. I know that doesn't matter during your hardest moments. To this day, when people tell me *this too shall pass*, I want to punch them in the face. That saying is bullshit. It's not helpful. So instead, I'll tell you this:

Some days will be harder than others. Some days will feel *really* long…some nights will feel even longer. There will be days where you feel like you didn't sign up for this at all and days where you lose your temper with your partner. There will be days you feel lost, days you feel lonely, and days where you miss the feeling of freedom and your old waist. There will be days when you want to throw your hands up and leave. You'll struggle for that day or that week, and you'll think, "I can't do it. This isn't what I expected. I don't think this mom thing is for me." And it's not because you're worried about what all of *this* is going to do to you, you're worried about what the hard days are going to do to *them*.

We worry about them. Sometimes, before they're even conceived, we worry about them. Where are they? When are they coming? What are we doing wrong? And then it happens. The stick turns pink, and for a moment, we feel calm. We feel a sense of control as we keep them safe inside. Watching what we eat, what we drink, and how we play. We're fixated on getting through those crucial first twelve weeks, seeing that little heartbeat flicker on the screen. Then the twelve weeks pass, and still, we worry about them. We count kicks and overthink movement. Anticipate fingers and toes. Every ache, pain, and symptom – we worry about them. In the way, only a mother can.

And then it happens. They enter our world like a force of nature. Capturing our hearts in an indescribable way. Life, I tell you, it's never the same after that. And despite fingers and toes, the colour of their hair, or their differences – to us, they are perfect. To us, they are no different. To us, they will conquer the world.

Yet, even with them safe in our embrace, we worry about them. We watch their breaths. We watch their weight. We watch their development. We follow charts and milestones. Wondering if we are doing enough, giving them enough, if to them – we are enough. We worry about them the way only a mother can. And this worry, ieighs heavily on a mama's heart. Because despite who they are, the challenges they face, or the way they came into our world – they are everything. And we want to protect them, wih every ounce of our being, every day of our life and beyond.

The worry that comes with being a mother is ingrained in us. It's what gives us superhuman strength, that pin-drop type of hearing, and the ability to see with eyes on the back of our head. It's why we stay up all night when we first bring them home, when they fight their first cold or get their first car. It's why we have a backup blankie in the closet, snacks in the fridge, and restrictions on the internet. It's because we worry. Because we want the best for them. Because we love them greater than life itself.

The thing about this type of worry – it may seem like a burden. To have a heaviness on your heart from the moment your baby takes their first breath to the moment you take your last. But I promise you – this worry comes with a certain kind of love. The love you experience from and for a child comes with no hesitation. It just is.

As an experienced parent, I've learned the value of waiting things out (with a carton of ice cream as my co-pilot). And I know that if I "just wait," the gong show will end for a few days at least, and eventually, we'll turn a corner. I know that if I "just wait," my sick and clingy toddler will soon start giggling and playing. I know that if I "just wait" for the sleep regression to pass, I'll become more patient with my kids and my husband. I know that if we "just wait" to make it out of this parenting lull, there will be beautiful periods to come. If we just wait, the clouds always break.

To any moms who are struggling, this book was written from a place of vulnerability, and I hope it strikes a chord within you. I hope it resonates with you on some level you have never tuned into before. I hope that it lifts you out of whatever challenge you're facing and helps you find a way back to the person you were placed on this earth to be.

When you're a mom – whether you're new at it or not – the day-in and day-out is hard. Loving as profoundly as we do, giving as much as we do, and being all that we are for those around us can suck our well dry. Sometimes there's nothing left to give ourselves. But there's a difference between motherhood being hard and motherhood feeling impossible. There's a difference between motherhood consuming your time and motherhood being all-consuming. And when you're finding life impossible and feeling all consumed, it's easy to blame yourself.

I sat on the floor across from my babies earlier tonight as they played cheerfully in the tub. We call bath time "Lawton Soup." There was music playing, and Dave was dancing. At one point, he scooped me off the floor and gave me a twirl. These days happen probably one percent of the time. Usually, I have to lure kids into the tub with a popsicle and hold them down while I wash their hair. But tonight, you guys – tonight was special. We listened to music, we danced, and my husband gave me a twirl. During that twirl, I caught a glimpse of myself in the mirror. I was laughing. There was a smile across my face and a smile in my eyes. I saw me. She's still in there.

It wasn't all that long ago that I was navigating motherhood with pieces of my heart broken and parts of my mind in disarray. My eyes showed a strange emptiness rather than life. The days were harder than I expected, and the nights were longer than I had hoped. But that's not where motherhood had lost me. I was lost in the feelings I couldn't shake, the panic I couldn't break, and the sadness that seeped through me like a poison—eroding my joy during what was supposed to be the most joyous moments of my life.

It took a long while for me to get to a place where I could twirl in a bathroom with a genuine smile on my face. It took me a long time to know that I wasn't okay. Today, there are still bits of me that are healing – but I'm present, I'm living, and there's no place I'd rather be. Except for when everyone is screaming. In those moments, I'd rather be 18 again with no responsibility, drinking jungle juice in a random field.

So, to the mom who didn't expect it to be like this – have hope. The twirl returns to your step.

25

YOU'VE DONE GOOD, MAMA.

The greatest and most important adventure in our lives is learning who we really are. And while it may sound like a self-centered goal, it truly is an unselfish process. There is no relationship more important than the relationship you have with yourself. If there's anything you take away from this book, I want that one sentence to be it. *There is no relationship more important than the relationship you have with yourself.*

I can only speak for myself, but I know I've spent my entire life trying to please other people. I tried to please the "cool" kids by changing my personality and trying to fit in, and I lost a piece of who I was. Then, I had sex for the first time with the wrong person, and I lost a part of who I was. I tried to pursue a certain career, not because I was passionate about it, but because I thought I would be more respected and successful - and I lost a piece of who I was. I spent twenty years losing bits and pieces of who I was. I chased happiness for so long that I never actually grew to understand what I needed to be happy. Then, I became a mom while not knowing I was a Swiss cheese version of myself. There were holes in my heart, my soul, and my self-confidence. And motherhood hit me hard. Having children didn't fill those holes. So, I panicked and frantically tried to find things to make me happy. But I didn't need happiness. The things that make us happy change all the time because we are changing all the time. What I needed was the wisdom that comes with aging and the confidence to live a life that represented me.

Our parents, friends, and even strangers provide us with wisdom. Some of the wisest words handed down to me are from those little old ladies that have crossed me in the line at the grocery store. *Time is precious.* They would tell me. *It passes fast.* They would say. *Those were some of the best days of my life.* These little old ladies weren't invested in my happiness. My life just happened to stir up memories for them, and they couldn't help but reminisce.

Just like they weren't invested in me, I'm not invested in you. Whether you want to be a piece of Swiss cheese or a piece of brie is a decision that you have to make. I will, however, tell you what I've learned from my own experience as a woman, a mother, and as a survivor of trauma. Because someone did it for me, and it changed the course of my life.

If you want to start filling in your holes, there's only one thing you need: life. Your lungs, your heart, your soul. You need nothing more than your two feet physically planted on the ground. A name-brand car with a leather interior or a big, luscious green front yard won't fill your holes. Family vacations, designer handbags, and a Pottery Barn bedroom for each of your kids in a Pinterest-worthy house won't fill your holes. They're nice to have. Girl, pin that shit and aspire to dream. But you don't *need* those things to be happier. And most importantly, your kids don't need those things.

One of the wisest things a mother from an older generation told me was that she understood my struggles but couldn't understand my wants. She knew what it was like to balance a career and understood the pressure of gender inequality. She knew mothers from her generation who had postpartum depression, were diagnosed with cancer, lost a parent or a spouse, had a neurodiverse child, or navigated financial woes. Those struggles are not new to our generation. But she couldn't understand all the extra noise. And she was really freaking sad that it was taking so much from us.

There's the noise that comes with social media, perfect white kitchens, trips to Disney, and the fucked up way it makes us believe that we need more of it. It bombards us from every direction and triggers those insecurities that make women feel like we're not doing enough. Motherhood comes to feel like a prison sentence. Which I know sounds harsh. But our generation of mothers have been taught that motherhood is to blame for how we look, for our careers falling apart, our marriages going to shit, and for not being able to look in the mirror and recognize ourselves. And yes, there is truth in that. Motherhood shakes things up. But man, our society wasn't built to support the twenty-first-century family. Women deserve way more credit. Ladies, it's not *you; it's them.* And by them, I mean unrealistic expectations. They trigger every insecurity we've gained along the way to motherhood.

The truth is, you are enough just as you are. You don't need to be anyone but yourself. If you try, you'll be met with disappointment when who you become doesn't feel "right." There's nothing wrong with ever wanting to be healthier, stronger, or more in tune with your true self – but that's the key to success. Don't work towards the person you want to be, work to uncover the person you know you are. Don't let Zuck or Pinterest, or TikTok make you think otherwise. Who you are is awesome, and your children need nothing more than your love. And if we put the same amount of effort into celebrating our wins as we do criticizing our losses, I don't think we'd look back so often, feeling like we missed out on them while trying so hard to provide for them.

Loving yourself doesn't happen overnight, and it's not even an everyday thing. But it has to start somewhere. You deserved a childhood, the same way your children are worthy of a childhood. As you work to create the perfect life for your children, you owe the little girl inside of you the opportunity to heal. It's a big ask. A responsibility the adults in your life left you with. But there is no way to move forward if you're still carrying hurt from your past.

Each and every one of us is a snowflake. Boomers, you're snowflakes too. We're all unique, we all have something to offer, and we're all here with a personal journey. No one emphasizes how important it is to remain authentic to that journey until it's almost too late. The more people you add to your life, the harder that healing journey becomes. I took my journey towards healing with a husband, two kids under two, and a Schnoodle under my roof. It wasn't easy – but if it wasn't for them, I'm not sure it ever would have happened.

That's kind of the crappiest part about this whole thing. Many of us don't realize how discombobulated we really are until we have kids of our own. And "self-care" is shoved down our throats like it's some sort of magic solution to healing. It's not. It takes way more than a yoga class every now and then. Though, I will say – I recently got my first Brazilian, and I've never felt more confident in my life. My vagina looks like a chicken breast, but some weird psychological magic is happening there.

Being a mother is something I've dreamed of since I was a little girl, and never in my mind or my heart did I anticipate motherhood would be the thing that resurfaced all of my trauma, insecurities, and failures. But when I think about it, it makes complete sense that motherhood is when most women fall apart. We're faced with this overwhelming love and responsibility to raise a child when there's a child inside all of us that never had the opportunity to grow up.

What they say is true, you know…you can't love someone until you love yourself. In the perspective of motherhood, you can't care for your babies until you care for yourself. You can't pour from an empty glass. You can't teach your children confidence and self-love, and self-worth if you have none of your own.

So, think about your life. Think about how you got to where you are today. Are you still carrying the baggage of your past with you? Is there hurt and depression, and anxiety buried somewhere deep within? Because I know motherhood isn't easy, and I know people say motherhood is where we get lost. But sometimes, it's exactly what we need to find our way back.

ABOUT THE AUTHOR

Anneliese Lawton is a Canadian gal with a big passion for maternal mental health. She had three kids in under four years and has lived to tell the tale. After reading dozens of self-help books, listening to podcasts, and writing for dozens of parenting publications-Anneliese learned that validation from other moms was key to feeling supported in motherhood. This mama of three (who wears far too many hats) is *Gabrielle Bernstein* meets *Workin' Moms* meets the *mom-next-door*. With her, nothing is off-limits, and she hopes her writing will inspire, empower and help other women find joy and peace within themselves.

CONNECT ONLINE

 @annielawton_

 grownupglamour

annielieselawton.com